Real World Mac Maintenance and Backups

Joe Kissell

Peachpit Press

Take Control Books

Real World Mac Maintenance and Backups

Joe Kissell

Peachpit Press
1249 Eighth Street
Berkeley, CA 94710
510/524-2178, 800/283-9444, 510/524-2221 (fax)

Find us on the Web at: www.peachpit.com
To report errors, please send a note to errata@peachpit.com

Peachpit Press is a division of Pearson Education

Real World Mac Maintenance and Backups is published in association with Take Control Books and was origi-nally published by Take Control Books as *Take Control of Maintaining Your Mac* (ISBN 1-933671-10-6) and *Take Control of Mac OS X Backups* (ISBN 0-9759503-0-4), both by Joe Kissell and copyright © 2006 by Joe Kissell. Learn more about Take Control at www.takecontrolbooks.com.

Copyright © 2007 by TidBITS Electronic Publishing and Joe Kissell

Editors: Jeff Carlson and Caroline Rose
Project Managers: Tonya Engst and Adam Engst
Production Editor: Susan Rimerman
Tech Editor: Take Control authors and the TidBITS Irregulars
Proofreader: Clark Humphrey
Compositor: Jeff Tolbert
Indexer: Rebecca Plunkett
Cover design: Aren Howell
Cover illustration: Alicia Buelow

Notice of Rights
All rights reserved. No part of this book may be reproduced or transmitted in any form by any means, electronic, mechanical, photocopying, recording, or otherwise, without the prior written permission of the publisher. For information on getting permission for reprints and excerpts, contact permissions@peachpit.com.

Notice of Liability
The information in this book is distributed on an "As Is" basis without warranty. While every precaution has been taken in the preparation of the book, neither the author nor Peachpit shall have any liability to any per-son or entity with respect to any loss or damage caused or alleged to be caused directly or indirectly by the instructions contained in this book or by the computer software and hardware products described in it.

Trademarks
Apple, FileVault, Finder, FireWire, iBook, iTunes, iTunes Music Store, Macintosh, .Mac, Mac, Mac OS, Panther, PowerBook, SuperDrive, and Tiger are trademarks or registered trademarks of Apple Computer, Inc.
Many of the designations used by manufacturers and sellers to distinguish their products are claimed as trademarks. Where those designations appear in this book, and Peachpit was aware of a trademark claim, the designations appear as requested by the owner of the trademark. All other product names and services iden-tified throughout this book are used in editorial fashion only and for the benefit of such companies with no intention of infringement of the trademark. No such use, or the use of any trade name, is intended to convey endorsement or other affiliation with this book.

ISBN 0-321-49218-8
9 8 7 6 5 4 3 2 1
Printed and bound in the United States of America

Overview

Contents

Introduction

A couple of years ago, I went to the dentist for the first time since the late 1990s. The main reason I'd failed to make dental appointments was embarrassment at having waited so long. I could just hear the dentist chiding me, "Ah, I can see you haven't had your teeth cleaned properly in 5 years. For shame!" The more time passed, the worse the embarrassment grew, and finally it took actual pain and a visible hole in a tooth to overcome it. So I was disappointed, but not surprised, to learn that I had several cavities and needed a root canal. The dentist was kind and understanding, but nevertheless pointed out several times that this visit might have been much less painful (and less expensive) had I flossed every day and gone for my semiannual checkups as I knew I should have.

I tell you this story not merely to urge proper dental hygiene, but because maintaining your Mac—like maintaining your teeth, your car, your health, or your home—is a good habit whose rewards are having fewer problems later on and being able to recover more easily from problems that do arise. You can sometimes get away without doing any maintenance for a few months or perhaps much longer, but you risk losing data, wasting time, and having to spend a great deal of money repairing or replacing your computer.

This book teaches you the most important and useful maintenance tasks you should perform to increase your chances of keeping your Mac in tip-top operating condition throughout its lifetime. I've organized the tasks according to their frequency: what you should do daily, weekly, monthly, and yearly, as well as some important initial steps, some things you should do when a Mac OS X upgrade appears, and some tasks you might want to *avoid,* contrary to conventional wisdom. Although no amount of maintenance can guarantee that nothing will go wrong with your computer, proper maintenance should minimize both the number and the severity of problems you experience.

Of course, disasters do sometimes occur: hard drives fail, computers are stolen or damaged, and files are accidentally deleted. Good backups are the best insurance against all these problems and more. If you've ever lost data—and I certainly have, on more than one occasion—then you know what I'm talking about. (And if you haven't lost data, you're computing on borrowed time.)

But when it comes to *how* to back up a computer, the options are so numerous that even the geekiest of us can find it difficult to wade through them and make intelligent choices. Which files should you back up? How often? Onto what media? Do you need to make bootable backups? How many sets of backup media do you need? Which backup software should you use? And what exactly do you do in case of a disaster, when you need to restore files from those backups? In the pages that follow, I offer some straightforward steps you can follow to come up with your own answers to these questions.

Regardless of the details of which hardware or software you use, your biggest concern should be *whether your data is safe.* What some people call a "backup" is simply copying files from your hard disk onto another volume—either manually or using a utility of some kind. I'm a firm believer in the principle that "something is better than nothing," so I don't want to make it sound as though this type of backup is useless. However, let me be candid: it's not enough. Too many different kinds of things can still imperil your data under such a scheme. A well-thought-out backup strategy will ensure the safety of your data—and helping you to develop such a strategy is one aim of this book.

Before we get started, I need to mention a few important disclaimers:

♦ There's no such thing as the One True Way to maintain or back up your Mac. Everyone's situation is unique, so you may need to adapt these instructions to suit your needs—perform certain tasks more often or less often, skip tasks that don't apply to you, and so on. Take these instructions as guidelines, as a starting point to determine your own maintenance regimen.

♦ I don't cover in any detail command-line software such as `diskutil`, `cp`, or `rsync`, except for a sidebar (see *Rolling Your Own with Unix Utilities*, page 150). Although such tools can certainly be used to perform maintenance and backups, my goal is to make the process as simple as possible—ideally without requiring you to open Terminal or know anything about Unix. So this book concerns itself strictly with software that uses a graphical user interface (GUI).

♦ I've written the backup chapters of this book primarily for people who need to back up either a single computer or a small network—not for system administrators who need to back up dozens or hundreds of machines. As a result, I say little about the expensive, high-end equipment typically used for backing up large networks, focusing instead on simpler devices you can purchase at your local computer store and plug directly into a stock Mac.

♦ Finally, this book does not cover troubleshooting or repair; the focus is on preventing problems, not fixing them. If your Mac crashes, fails to start up, or otherwise behaves improperly, you'll need to look elsewhere for solutions. (I recommend some places to look in Appendix A.)

Note: To reflect the diversity of opinion about certain maintenance tasks, I've included several sidebars containing brief conversations among Mac experts, most of whom are authors or editors. These discussions are based on comments made on a preliminary draft of this book.

Although I wrote this book based on Mac OS X 10.4 Tiger, most of the information should apply equally well to earlier and later versions of Mac OS X. (One of the first suggestions I make is to upgrade your Mac, if possible, to run the latest version of Mac OS X, which is likely to contain fewer bugs than earlier versions.) Likewise, most of this material applies in a general way to machines running Mac OS 9 and Windows. I don't cover these other operating systems in any detail, but do see *Windows Files Backup Strategy* (page 114), which discusses backing up Windows when it's running on your Intel-based Mac.

The tasks in this book are easy, and they get easier the more you do them. So start developing those good maintenance and backup habits right now. And don't forget to floss every day!

Basics

In reading this book, you may get stuck if you don't know certain basic facts about Mac OS X, or if you don't understand my syntax for things like working with menus or finding items in the Finder. Please note the following:

♦ **Path syntax:** This book occasionally uses a *path* to show the location of a file or folder in your file system. For example, Mac OS X stores most utilities, such as Terminal, in the Utilities folder. The path to Terminal is: /Applications/Utilities/Terminal.

The slash at the start of the path tells you to start from the root level of the disk. You will also encounter paths that begin with ~ (tilde), which is a shortcut for any user's home directory. For example, if a person with the user name joe wants to install fonts that only he can access, he would install them in his ~/Library/Fonts folder, which is just another way of writing /Users/joe/Library/Fonts.

♦ **Menus:** When I describe choosing a command from a menu in the menu bar, I use an abbreviated description. For example, the abbreviated description for the menu command that creates a new folder in the Finder is "File > New Folder."

♦ **Finding preference panes:** I sometimes refer to systemwide Mac OS X preferences that you may want to adjust. To change these settings, open System Preferences by clicking its icon in the Dock or choosing System Preferences from the Apple menu. Settings are categorized into topic-specific *preference panes.* You access a particular preference pane by way of its icon or the View menu. For example, to see "the .Mac preference pane," you would launch System Preferences and then click the .Mac icon or choose View > .Mac.

Acknowledgments

I'd like to thank my editors, Caroline Rose and Jeff Carlson, for their outstanding and speedy work in preparing the text of this book for publication. I appreciate the tremendous effort Adam Engst and Tonya Engst put into making this book a reality, as well as Jeff Tolbert's superb layout work, Clark Humphrey's proofreading, and Rebecca Plunkett's indexing. Special thanks to all the Control Freaks and TidBITS Irregulars who reviewed this book and provided numerous (sometimes very passionate) suggestions. In particular, I want to acknowledge those who graciously agreed to include reasonable facsimiles of their comments here: Andy Affleck, Sharon Zardetto Aker, Geoff Duncan, Adam Engst, Tonya Engst, Glenn Fleishman, Dan Frakes, Peter N Lewis, Kirk McElhearn, and Chris Pepper. Finally, thanks to Nancy Davis and Susan Rimerman at Peachpit Press for making this book possible.

Colophon

Software: This book was written and edited in Microsoft Word, versions X and 2004 (depending on who was writing or editing), and laid out in Adobe InDesign from Creative Suite 2. Screenshots were captured with Ambrosia Software's Snapz Pro X. Backups of the work in progress were made by Retrospect Desktop.

Fonts: The body text is Utopia (from Adobe); titles and subheads are in Optima (also from Adobe); the monospaced font for pathnames and URLs has the strange name TheSansMonoCondensed (from the also strangely named Luc(as) De Groot).

Quick Start

This book describes a step-by-step process for maintaining and backing up your Mac. The maintenance intervals (daily, weekly, monthly, yearly) reflect the relative urgency of the tasks in each section; you may choose to do the tasks within a section in any order, but I strongly suggest first following the steps in Chapter 1.

Get ready:

♦ Get your Mac into the best possible shape by updating your software, getting rid of old files, and performing other preliminary tasks. Read Chapter 1.

Perform periodic maintenance tasks:

♦ Every day, update your backup archive and download (but don't necessarily install) software updates. See Chapter 2.

♦ Once each week, perform maintenance such as cleaning up your Desktop, backing up your hard drive, installing software updates, and rebooting or clearing certain caches if you notice performance problems. See Chapter 3.

◆ Once a month, empty your Trash, check your disk for errors, do some light cleaning, and exercise your notebook's battery. See Chapter 4.

◆ Once a year, give your Mac a good spring cleaning inside and out; make extra backups for long-term storage, get rid of extraneous files, and change your passwords. See Chapter 5.

Save time by skipping unnecessary work:

◆ Learn why you can probably avoid two common maintenance tasks. Read Chapter 6.

Handle Mac OS X upgrades with ease:

◆ Before you know it, Apple will ship the next major upgrade to Mac OS X. Learn what you need to know to be ready for it in Chapter 7.

Avoid or fix problems:

◆ Catch hardware and software problems before they become serious, or troubleshoot them if they do happen. See Chapter 8 and Appendix A.

Decide on a backup strategy:

Read Chapter 9 to understand the rationale behind the hardware, software, and setup advice I give later.

◆ Understand the crucial differences between a duplicate and an archive, and why a good backup strategy includes both. See *The Duplicate* (page 92) and *The Archive* (page 94).

◆ Learn the most effective and the least difficult ways to back up your photos and videos. First read *Do You Have Special Backup Needs?* (page 90), and then see *Digital Photos* (page 90) and *Video and Audio* (page 91).

◆ Learn the value of using a single system to back up all the Macs in your home or office. See *Backing Up a Small Network* (page 99).

Choose your backup hardware:

◆ Learn the pros and cons of each media type (from CD-R to camcorders) and how to estimate the amount of storage space you'll need. See Chapter 10.

Choose your backup software:

◆ Find out what to look for when comparing backup applications. See Chapter 11 for a feature overview, and then consult Appendix B for details and sources.

Set up your backup system:

In Chapter 12 we put all the pieces together and get your backup system running smoothly.

◆ Make a bootable copy of your hard disk and test it to make sure it works. See *Set Up Duplicates* (page 163) and *Test Your Duplicate* (page 165).

◆ Configure an archive for your most frequently used data files, and verify that you can retrieve stored files. See *Set Up Archives* (page 167) and *Test Your Archive* (page 169).

◆ Put your backups on autopilot so that your files are protected even when you aren't paying attention. See *Automate Your Backups* (page 170).

◆ Learn how and where to store backup media, and what to do with the media when it gets full. See *Mind Your Media* (page 172).

◆ If disaster strikes and you need to recover files, be sure you're familiar with the steps in *Restore Data from a Backup* (page 177).

◆ Do you use Retrospect as your backup software? If so, read the detailed instructions for major Retrospect tasks in Appendix C.

Tip: If you want to see a very funny video about the importance of backups, featuring none other than John Cleese (The Minister of Silly Walks, Q, Nearly Headless Nick, and so on), visit LiveVault's Web site at `www.backuptrauma.com/video/default2.aspx`. (LiveVault sells Internet-based backup systems to businesses—but unfortunately, their products don't run on Macs.)

Start on the Right Foot

Whether you've just unpacked a shiny new Mac or you're hoping to get an older machine into shape, your first step should be to perform some initial cleanup and preparation tasks. These steps will help your Mac run better right now, and will make ongoing maintenance tasks easier.

Install the Latest Version of Mac OS X

If your Mac is already running the latest and greatest version of Mac OS X, good for you! Skip to the next section. If not, your first step should be to upgrade.

Every release of Mac OS X includes dozens if not hundreds of bug fixes that prevent crashes or other errors and that patch holes that ne'er-do-wells might use to damage or gain access to your system. That fact alone is reason enough to keep up to date. In addition, Apple constantly introduces useful new features, and some newer software runs only on recent versions of the operating system. Often, doing nothing more than updating your system software can eliminate a wide range of problems—and prevent others.

Mac OS X updates fall into two categories: major and minor. Major updates (more properly known as upgrades) increment the digit after the first decimal point in the version number: 10.2, 10.3, and 10.4 were all major updates. With rare exceptions, Apple charges money (typically $129) for major updates. Minor updates increment the digit after the second decimal point: 10.4.2, 10.4.3, and 10.4.4 were all minor updates. Minor updates are always free.

Without exception, you should download and install every minor update. (I do, however, suggest waiting a few days after an update appears to make sure it doesn't contain any serious errors.) The easiest way to do so is to use Software Update (see the next section). Major upgrades are less urgent, because they focus primarily on new features. But because they also fix numerous bugs, you should consider buying and installing them.

Some Mac users, having heard horror stories of half-baked releases that cause as many problems as they fix, feel anxious every time a software update appears. I won't lie to you: major errors occasionally sneak into system updates. But this happens rarely, and in most cases Apple resolves such problems promptly. In addition, a fair number of errors that appear to be update-related are in fact the result of existing problems on the user's machine, minor issues such as incorrect permissions, or even (gasp!) user errors. I can't guarantee that a software update will never break anything, but in my experience the benefits of incremental updates overwhelmingly outweigh the risks—especially if you maintain good backups.

Turn On Software Update

Mac OS X includes a feature called Software Update, which checks Apple's servers periodically to see if free updates exist for any Apple software on your computer, and, if so, offers to download and install them for you. Software Update is the easiest way to keep your Mac up to date with bug fixes and minor enhancements, and I strongly recommend that you use it.

Note: I want to reiterate that Software Update handles only Apple software (including Mac OS X as well as applications such as iLife, iWork, Logic, and Aperture). To learn how to update third-party software, see *Update Third-Party Software* (page 15).

Software Update is enabled by default, but you should check to see that it's still on and that its options are configured optimally. To set up Software Update, follow these steps:

1. Go to the Software Update pane of System Preferences (**Figure 1**).

Figure 1

Configure Software Update settings in this preference pane.

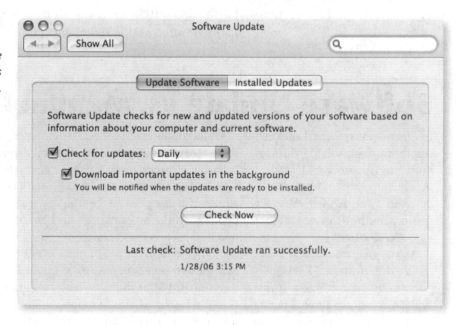

2. Make sure the Check for Updates checkbox is checked. Then, from the pop-up menu, choose how often Software Update should run: Daily, Weekly, or Monthly. (If you have an always-on, high-speed Internet connection, choose Daily; even if you choose not to install an update immediately, you'll know about it as soon as possible.)

3. If you have a fast Internet connection and plenty of disk space, check Download Important Updates in the Background. This causes Software Update to download things like Mac OS X updates and security updates as soon as it sees them. You still get to choose whether or not

to install them, but when you do choose, you don't have to wait for the download to complete—the files are there, ready to go.

4. To perform an immediate check, click Check Now. Software Update informs you if any new software is available. (You can also check for updates at any time by choosing Software Update from the Apple menu.)

5. Close System Preferences.

At the interval you set, Software Update checks for new software. When it finds some, it displays a dialog in which you can select any or all of the updates for immediate installation, defer them to a later time, or remove items from the list entirely. For complete details, read *Use Software Update to Install Apple Software Updates* (page 42).

Software Update vs. Manual Updates

In general, software packages that Apple makes available through Software Update are also available on the company's Web site, so you can download them manually if you wish from www.apple.com/support/downloads/.

Starting with the second minor release of each Mac OS X version—such as 10.4.2 for Tiger—Apple typically produces three separate updaters: the updater available only through Software Update, known as a "patch" or "smaller-sized delta" updater; the standard (or "regular-sized delta") updater; and the "combo" updater.

Delta updaters require the most recent previous release to be installed; for example, a 10.4.6 updater would require that 10.4.5 already be installed. A combo updater, on the other hand, will update any previous version of the major system release (in this example, any release from 10.4.0 through 10.4.5) to the new version. Because of this, combo updaters are always larger—in some cases *much* larger. Software Update chooses the smallest applicable updater, which means it chooses the smaller-sized delta updater if you run Software Update regularly.

Why should you care? Well, on a few occasions, users have found that using the delta updaters (whether manually or via Software Update) for some reason left out essential files that prevented proper operation of some Mac OS X features, whereas these files *were* included when the same users applied the combo updater.

Although I've never had problems with the delta updaters, anecdotal evidence suggests that you may have a slightly lower risk of problems if you manually download the combo updater for each Mac OS X update instead of using Software Update.

Update Third-Party Software

Software bugs are a fact of life, but in general, applications improve with each release. You can avoid, or solve, many maintenance problems simply by making sure you have the latest version of every program installed.

Note: In some cases, getting the latest version of a program means spending hundreds of dollars on a major upgrade. In cases where you can't afford the absolutely latest version, you should at least install the latest free update you can find. This may require some searching on the company's Web site; earlier updates may not be featured as prominently as the most recent update.

Because Software Update handles only Apple software, any other developer wanting to offer similar capabilities must devise a separate update mechanism. Happily, almost every major application (and a good percentage of minor ones) contains some sort of software update feature. Unhappily, they don't all work the same way. Some of them check for updates on a schedule, while others don't—and of those that do, not all have this feature turned on initially. Some programs can download *and* install new versions of themselves automatically, while others simply download a disk image and expect you to open it and run the installer yourself; still others do nothing but open a Web page with links to updates you can download manually.

In an ideal world, updates would require no intervention other than a single click to confirm that you're aware of, and approve of, the installation; everything else would happen automagically. Because only a few applications currently offer that level of automation, though, you may have to perform some extra steps.

I describe how to handle ongoing updates ahead. For now, do just two things:

♦ **Make sure all your software is currently up to date.** In each of the applications you use frequently, look for a Check for Updates command (the wording may vary). Such commands usually appear in the application menu (the one bearing the application's name), the Help menu, or the Preferences dialog. If you can't find such a command, visit the developer's Web site.

Don't forget: Be sure to check for updates of preference panes, menu extras, plug-ins, Dashboard widgets, and other system enhancements. These types of software frequently lack an automatic update feature.

♦ **Turn on any automatic software update features your applications may have.** Again, check each application's Preferences dialog for a checkbox that enables scheduled updates, and if you can choose how often to check, choose the most frequent option.

Gripe: Some applications check for updates every time you launch them, and display an intrusive alert after each check just to tell you that no updates are available. Ugh! An alert of that sort should appear only after a manual check for updates. In such cases, I either turn off automatic checking or change it to a weekly or monthly check.

Clean Out Accumulated Cruft

The term "cruft" is hacker slang for digital detritus—obsolete, extraneous, or otherwise useless files that have accumulated on your disk over time and now do nothing but take up space. By removing cruft, you can recover valuable disk space, increase the speed of backups, file searches, upgrades, and disk diagnostics, and reduce the chance of software conflicts. If you have a brand-new Mac, this step may not apply to you, but even a few months of use can generate a surprising amount of cruft.

Determining which files you need and which can go may be a nontrivial undertaking. Some files ("My 2006 tax deductions.xls" or "Take Control of Maintaining Your Mac.pdf") are obviously important, and some (caches, old downloads, and so on) are obviously disposable. In between you may find thousands of files that you can't identify and that may or may not have some value.

My advice is to work slowly and deliberately, and avoid deleting anything whose purpose you're uncertain about. In particular—with only a few exceptions I'll mention shortly—you should be circumspect about deleting things in /Library, and almost never delete anything in /System. And remember: this is something you do to reduce clutter, not a matter of life or death. So don't be too ruthless when it comes to deleting files.

Back up first: *Because you're about to delete files, I strongly recommend that you make a full backup first, in case you accidentally delete something important. See* Create a Backup System *(page 22) and* Back Up Everything *(page 41).*

Here are my suggestions for files you might consider deleting:

♦ Your ~/Documents folder is a likely place for unneeded files. Skim the contents of this folder and its subfolders, looking for documents and application support files you no longer need, and drag such items to the Trash.

Tip: Numerous programs make automatic backups of their files. This is a good thing, but over time you might accumulate dozens or hundreds of old, large backup files that do you no good. BBEdit and MYOB AccountEdge are examples of programs that tend to generate large numbers of backup files.

In addition, if you save iChat transcripts (in ~/Documents/iChats), you might also wish to delete old ones. And Eudora users may want to look through ~/Documents/Eudora Folder/Attachments Folder for unneeded attachments.

♦ Look in /Applications (and /Applications/Utilities) for any software you've installed over the past year but never use. (Expired demo software, anyone?) Resist the temptation to delete Apple software that came with Mac OS X, though; you may need it later.

♦ In the folders /Library, /Library/Application Support, ~/Library, and ~/Library/Application Support, look for folder names matching applications you no longer use, and delete them.

♦ Your /Library and ~/Library folders may hold other folders that store components of third-party utilities. Look inside the folders called

Application Enhancers, Bundles, Contextual Menu Items, InputManagers, and PreferencePanes for any system enhancements you no longer use, and drag them to the Trash.

◆ Third-party Dashboard widgets live in ~/Library/Widgets. Any widgets you don't use can go.

◆ Software that requires some component to be running in the background all the time may install folders in /Library/StartupItems. In most cases, you should leave this folder alone, but if you see anything there from software you're sure you don't use, delete it.

Warning! *The* /Library/StartupItems *folder often contains background software you need but weren't aware you needed. For example, SOHO Notes uses an item in this folder called OpenBase; Retrospect uses a folder named RetroRun; and Now Up-to-Date & Contact uses a folder named NUDC. In short, if you're uncertain about anything in this folder, don't touch it.*

A Conversation about Removing Cruft

How important is it to remove extraneous files? These experts expressed a variety of opinions:

Kirk McElhearn: One thing I do is remove language files (using Monolingual, http://monolingual.sourceforge.net/) every once in a while. It saves a bit of disk space and makes backups a little faster.

Glenn Fleishman: I think advice to remove cruft is very 1990s. There's little reason, except for backup storage issues and local storage issues, to ever delete a document. Movies and pictures may need extra storage or culling, but between Spotlight searching and giant hard drives, why delete? Backups are only marginally slower with a greater number of small

files, so the advantage in deleting them is minimal.

Kirk McElhearn: You can save more than 1 GB by deleting language files, and this allows you to make a clone on a smaller partition for backups.

Joe Kissell: I don't delete language files myself, because I have plenty of disk space and I don't like to muck around with applications unnecessarily. However, to Glenn's point, I think removing cruft is valid even if you have tons of disk space, and Spotlight searching is in fact a great example of why I think that: when I'm looking for a file, I don't want to have to wade through a long list of matches, most of which are irrelevant items I could have deleted. And backups

may not take much longer if you're backing up to another hard disk, but if you're backing up to optical media or a network server, every extra gigabyte has a significant impact.

Tonya Engst: I think it depends on the person. For example, I hate to keep extra email. It bothers me to have crufty mailboxes. I think it's OK for people to figure out whether they're pack rats or not, and to behave accordingly. I have found, though, that the better my filing scheme, the more files I keep. What I hate are files whose purpose or contents I can't easily identify. It's like someone else (perhaps Apple) putting real clutter on my real office shelves.

◆ Kernel extensions (files with names ending in .kext) add low-level functionality to Mac OS X. Examples include hardware drivers (for devices such as mice, trackballs, and audio interfaces), encryption tools, and screen-capture software. These files are stored in either /Library/Extensions or /System/Library/Extensions. Any such software you no longer need can be deleted, but be *very* careful, especially in /System/Library/Extensions: most of these files are essential to Mac OS X, and that includes some that may have a third-party company in their name. If you see any obsolete items in one of these folders, the safest way to remove them is to run the installer that put them there in the first place and choose Uninstall (or follow uninstallation instructions provided by the developer). Do not delete them manually.

Tip: Uninstaller Utilities. If you prefer not to muck around in your Library folders looking for individual files to delete, consider picking up a utility that can do all the hard work for you. Here are some examples:

◆ **Spring Cleaning:** This utility from Allume (www.allume.com; $50) can find and remove all sorts of cruft, including empty folders, orphaned aliases, Internet caches, and of course ordinary applications and their supporting files. Among the many tricks up its sleeve is the ability to restore items it has deleted if you later realize that you need them.

◆ **AppZapper:** A much simpler tool, AppZapper (www.appzapper.com; $13) does just one thing (and does it well): it removes all the pieces associated with a given application, including preference and cache files, items in your Application Support folders, and even installer receipt files.

I should also mention two utilities that don't make any attempt to uninstall software but simply help you identify and delete large files on your drive that you may not need:

◆ **OmniDiskSweeper:** (www.omnigroup.com; $15)

◆ **WhatSize:** (www.id-design.com/software/; free)

When you're finished deleting files, be sure to empty the Trash (Finder > Empty Trash) to recover the space the files previously occupied.

Turn Off Unneeded Login Items

Mac OS X can run applications or open files automatically when any given user logs in; items set to open in this way are called *login items*. (Under Mac OS X 10.3 Panther, Apple called them *startup items*.) You can add a login item manually—for example, to save yourself a click or two by making sure your email program or Web browser runs every time you log in. Numerous applications also install login items—often without advertising that fact—so that background services they rely on are always available. Examples of programs that install background-only login items are iCal, Microsoft Office, Quicken, and StuffIt Deluxe.

Login items are useful, but they can also increase the time it takes to start your Mac (or switch users). In addition, the more applications you have running at once, the greater your RAM usage and CPU load. So I recommend checking to make sure you don't have any login items you can do without.

To check your login items, follow these steps:

1. Go to the Accounts pane of System Preferences.

2. Select your account in the list on the left and click the Login Items button (**Figure 2**).

3. Scan the list of login items for any you no longer use. If you find one, select it and click the ⊟ button. (This removes the item from the list but does not delete the corresponding file from your disk.) Repeat as necessary.

Tip: If you hover your mouse pointer over an item in the Login Items list for a few seconds, a yellow tool tip appears with that item's complete path. This information may not tell you exactly what the item does, but it at least tells you where it is, which may provide important clues.

Figure 2

In the Login Items view, look for login items you no longer need and remove them.

You may find a few unfamiliar items in the Login Items list that are nevertheless legitimate and useful. In particular, do not remove these items, if present:

♦ **iCalAlarmScheduler:** Enables iCal to display alarms even when the application is not running.

♦ **iTunesHelper:** Watches for an iPod being connected or disconnected, to help iTunes communicate with it.

♦ **Microsoft AU Daemon:** Schedules automatic updates for Microsoft Office applications.

♦ **System Events:** Enables AppleScript (or applications based on Apple-Script) to send commands to parts of the operating system.

Create a Backup System

No amount of maintenance can guarantee that your hard drive will never crash, that your Mac will never be stolen, or that lightning will never hit your house. Any number of catastrophes could potentially imperil your computer—and its data. Of course, you can replace a computer, but what about your email, photographs, music collection, tax records, and all the other important information on your hard disk? To keep your data safe, you need good backups. If you've never taken the time to set up a proper backup system, the time is now!

I wish I could tell you that backing up your computer is a simple matter of clicking a few buttons. But there's more to it than that: understanding the various types of backup, choosing backup hardware and software that has all the features you need, configuring your system, storing backup media safely, and many other details. The good news, though, is that once you've set up a backup system, it should run happily with little intervention for months or years.

Because so much can be said about backups, I've devoted several later chapters of this book to providing you with complete instructions. Feel free to work your way through the tasks in the rest of this book first. When you're ready to set up your backup system, flip ahead to Chapter 9, where you'll begin to learn how to choose backup hardware and software, schedule daily archives and weekly duplicates, manage your media, and more. If you set everything up now, you'll breeze through those periodic tasks, almost without noticing them.

Run Apple Hardware Test

When you purchased your Macintosh, the box should have included a CD or DVD with an application called Apple Hardware Test. Depending on when you bought your computer, this could be an independent disc, or it may be included on the Mac OS X Install Disc. (Look for tiny lettering on the disc that says "To use Apple Hardware Test, hold down the Option key as the computer starts up," or words to that effect.) Find this disc now.

(I'll wait while you root through your attic or basement to find it hidden in the bottom of a box somewhere.)

Back already? Super. You have in your hands a very special program. Apple Hardware Test can run only when you start up from the CD or DVD it came on; don't bother trying to copy it to your hard disk. This program performs a series of diagnostic tests on your Mac's hardware, including the AirPort card, logic board, hard drive, RAM, modem, and video RAM. It doesn't repair anything, and it doesn't look for problems such as directory errors that are the province of Disk Utility (described in the next section). But it can identify subtle hardware defects that could later lead to serious problems. Whether your Mac is fresh out of the box or years old, you owe it to yourself to make sure its major components are in good health, and this is the easiest (and cheapest) way to do so.

Note: Apple Hardware Test isn't the only tool that can check your RAM. Among the other utilities that can do this are TechTool Pro (www.micromat.com; $98) and Rember (www.kelleycomputing.net/rember/; free). I've personally had bad RAM that Apple Hardware Test could identify while these others could not, whereas other Take Control authors have had the opposite experience. Your mileage may vary!

To run Apple Hardware Test, follow these steps:

1. Insert the disc with Apple Hardware Test on it into your Mac and restart, holding down the Option key until icons appear representing the available startup volumes.

2. Click the Apple Hardware Test icon, and then click the right arrow.

3. After the program loads, select a language and click the right arrow.

4. On the Hardware Tests tab, click Extended Test.

5. Take a nice hot bath or enjoy a stroll around your neighborhood. This test takes a while! The screen says, "Estimated time: 10–15 minutes, or longer depending on the amount of memory installed." Take the "or longer" part seriously. On a fairly fast test machine with 2 GB of RAM, the test took almost an hour and 45 minutes.

6. If all is well, the word "Passed" appears next to all the applicable tests in the Test Results area. If not, a failure message appears; if this happens, look in the About the Test and Results area for advice.

7. Click Restart to restart your computer.

I recommend running the test again after installing RAM or any other new hardware inside your computer, or if you begin to have inexplicable problems that ordinary disk utilities do not solve.

Be Sure You Have Enough RAM

The most important thing you can do to speed up your Mac and reduce crashes is to be sure it contains enough RAM. Few new Macs ship with what I consider "enough." Even though Mac OS X and most applications can run in as little as 512 MB, in my experience performance degrades quickly with that amount of RAM when you have numerous applications and windows open at once.

How much RAM *should* you have? The answer depends on the type of Mac, the way you work, and your budget. On the one hand, I think everyone should have at least 1 GB (or the maximum their machine supports, if less). On the other hand, more isn't necessarily better. For example, only a few people running the most memory-intensive applications would benefit from putting the maximum of 16 GB in a Power Mac G5.

In general, if your Mac can hold 2 GB or less, I recommend maxing it out (budget permitting). Go above 2 GB if you spend all day working with heavy-duty photo, video, or audio applications, if you run high-end scientific software that performs complex mathematical operations, or if your computer functions as a server in a high-demand environment.

Run Disk Utility

You know the old saying: "If it ain't broke, don't fix it!" With computers, though, things can be broken without manifesting any obvious symptoms. You can nip many such problems in the bud with a simple procedure that looks for, and fixes, common disk errors that can crop up over time without your knowledge. I recommend doing this not only as an initial step, but also monthly.

To repair your disk, follow these steps:

1. Start up your Mac from media *other than* your regular startup disk that also contains Disk Utility. This could be, for example:

    ♦ A bootable duplicate of your startup disk stored on an external FireWire hard drive (or a USB 2.0 hard drive, if you have an Intel-based Mac), a second internal drive, or a second partition of your main disk

    ♦ A Mac OS X installation DVD or CD

    ♦ A TechTool Protégé device, to which you've copied Disk Utility (www.micromat.com)

    Note: You can't repair the disk from which Mac OS X is running (or the disk from which Disk Utility is running, if it's not the same one); that would be somewhat like trying to perform brain surgery on yourself. You can, however, verify the disk (by clicking Verify Disk in Step 4) to determine whether there are problems that Disk Utility could repair.

    ---

2. Run Disk Utility. (If running from a cloned hard disk, you can find it in /Applications/Utilities. If running from a Mac OS X installation disc, click through the language selection screen and then choose Utilities > Disk Utility.)

3. In the list on the left side of the window, select your main startup volume (the one you want to test), as in **Figure 3**.

4. On the First Aid tab, click Repair Disk.

Disk Utility looks for common errors and repairs them if possible. Ordinarily, it displays a message saying that repairs were completed or that no repairs were necessary. In the (rare) event that Disk Utility encounters a serious problem it cannot solve, you may need to use a commercial repair tool such as DiskWarrior (www.alsoft.com; $80).

Figure 3

Select a volume (other than the startup volume) on the left, and then click Repair Disk.

Make Sure Scheduled Maintenance Tasks Run

Mac OS X includes a tiny Unix utility called periodic whose purpose is to perform a variety of cleanup tasks, such as deleting old log files that would otherwise take up unnecessary space on your disk and updating the index that the Unix locate command uses to find files in the Terminal utility. The periodic utility can perform any of three sets of tasks. Once a day, periodic is supposed to run "daily" tasks; once a week, "weekly" tasks; and once a month, "monthly" tasks. (These names are more or less arbitrary; if, for example, you ran the monthly tasks every week, no harm would result.)

The `periodic` program doesn't launch itself, though; running it at the proper times is the job of another program, called `launchd` (under Tiger; in earlier versions of Mac OS X a utility called `cron` told `periodic` when to run). Apple set the launchers to run the `periodic` scripts in the middle of the night, so that they wouldn't slow down other things your Mac might be doing. The problem is that if your Mac happens to be off or asleep at the scheduled time (as it is for most of us), the scripts can't run. Tiger's `launchd` utility was supposed to be smart enough to notice that it had missed a scheduled task and run it the next time your Mac became active. Unfortunately, as of Mac OS X 10.4.4, `launchd` is flaky: sometimes the `periodic` scripts run (though possibly at completely unpredictable times) and sometimes they don't.

Tip: To learn more about `launchd`, which is quite useful despite its limitations, see an article I wrote for *Macworld* magazine: "Launch Your Mac" at `www.macworld.com/2006/01/secrets/februarygeekfactor/`.

In short, unless you leave your Macintosh on and awake all the time, the `periodic` command needs a bit of help to do its thing. The easiest solution is to download any of several programs that enable you to run the maintenance scripts manually at any time or, in some cases, to schedule them for times you know your Mac will be available. Try one of these:

- **Anacron:** This free utility runs the maintenance scripts whenever they're overdue, with no user intervention required. You can find it at `http://members.cox.net/18james/anacron-tiger.html`.

- **Cocktail:** Cocktail (`www.maintain.se/cocktail/`; $15), shown in **Figure 4**, provides a single, simple interface for performing a wide range of maintenance tasks, including running the maintenance scripts, deleting cache files and old logs, adjusting hidden Finder, Dock, Safari, and Exposé settings, and more. Some tasks can run on a recurring schedule.

- **Mac HelpMate:** This utility (`www.macworkshops.com/machelpmate/`; free, donations accepted) can run the maintenance scripts manually or on a schedule. It also deletes various caches, adjusts hidden Finder and Dock settings, displays your drives' S.M.A.R.T. status (see *Check Your*

Drives' S.M.A.R.T. Status, page 82), disk usage and system uptime, and performs numerous other maintenance tasks.

Figure 4

Cocktail's System pane contains controls for running the daily, weekly, and monthly maintenance scripts. You can also use the Pilot pane to schedule them to run automatically.

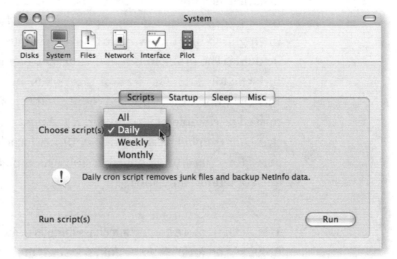

- ◆ **MacJanitor:** If you want nothing more than a simple utility that lets you run the daily, weekly, and monthly maintenance scripts manually, the free MacJanitor (`http://personalpages.tds.net/%7ebrian_hill/macjanitor.html`) does that nicely.

- ◆ **MainMenu:** Like most of the other utilities in this list, MainMenu (`www.santasw.com`; free, donations accepted) performs a wide variety of functions, including running the maintenance scripts, clearing caches, and deleting log files. Unlike the others, it puts all these commands into a single, always-accessible menu, so that you can run any of them with a single click.

- ◆ **OnyX:** Another multipurpose utility, the free OnyX can run the maintenance scripts manually (but not on a schedule), delete various caches and log files, adjust hidden Finder, Dock, and Safari settings, display log files, run Unix commands, and display disk usage and system uptime, among other tasks (`www.titanium.free.fr/pgs/english.html`).

Warning! *The utilities I list here are among dozens of tools that provide a pretty GUI wrapper to Unix commands. With all such programs, you should be careful not to click buttons blindly; because Unix commands can theoretically do just about anything, you could cause damage if you don't know what you're doing.*

Install Antivirus Software

If this book were about PC maintenance, one of the first steps would have been to install antivirus software. For Windows users, malicious software (or *malware*) has become epidemic in recent years, leading to untold grief and loss of time, money, and data. Among the varieties of malware are viruses (and their close cousins *worms* and *Trojan horses*), *spyware* (programs that spy on your computer usage, collecting sensitive personal data), and pop-up ad programs. Luckily, very little malware runs on Mac OS X: as of the time I wrote this, I could count on one hand the programs of this sort that have been found "in the wild."

Even though Mac users have been fortunate so far, we would be wrong to assume our computers are immune to infection. Sooner or later, someone is bound to come up with malicious software that does serious damage to Macs, and when that happens, those with enough foresight to have installed antivirus software will be much more likely to continue merrily with their work while the rest of us struggle to restore our systems.

A Conversation about Periodic Maintenance Tasks

Should you worry about running the periodic maintenance tasks at all? The experts had this to say:

Kirk McElhearn: This is one of my bugbears. In very few cases are these routines essential and, with all due respect, I think it's excessive to suggest otherwise. Too many users think that these routines can solve problems; I've never seen a case where this is true. At best—unless you use the `locate` command—they're placebos. They can clean out some log files, but again, only in some cases (if you run a server) does this make much of a difference.

Andy Affleck: I've found that the real advantage to running these tasks regularly is the log rotation. When I ran them manually I saw some space gains on my disk. It wasn't huge, but it was noticeable.

Dan Frakes: I agree with Andy: for most people it won't help much, but it will clean up log files. And if you use `locate`—or the free GUI equivalent, Locator (www.sebastian-krauss.de/software/)—it's useful to have the `locate` database updated regularly.

Chris Pepper: Right, and remember, the `locate` database is as relevant to SSH or a BBEdit shell worksheet as it is to Terminal.

Joe Kissell: I use `locate` all the time, so this is a big deal to me. For what it's worth, updating the `locate` database is one of the *weekly* script items. All three script types (daily, weekly, and monthly) rotate certain logs. The daily tasks also back up your NetInfo database and delete certain "scratch" files, such as temporary files used when you send faxes. The monthly tasks include generating reports of system usage for each user.

Furthermore, many kinds of malware spread via email, so you could unwittingly serve as a carrier by forwarding messages containing viruses to your Windows-using friends.

Your best defense is to load antivirus software—*and keep it up to date*. Developers release regular updates (to handle the latest threats), and you must be certain to configure your preferences to download them automatically as soon as they appear.

Note: Although having antivirus software is better than not having it, and having up-to-date antivirus software is better still, there are no ironclad guarantees. A particularly wily virus might still sneak by. So you should still exercise caution, and especially avoid opening iChat or email attachments from unknown sources.

Antivirus software available for Mac OS X includes the following:

♦ ClamXav (www.markallan.co.uk/clamXav/; free)

♦ Intego VirusBarrier X4 (www.intego.com; $70)

♦ Norton AntiVirus (www.symantec.com; $50)

Use a Surge Protector

If that AC cord coming out of your computer goes directly into a wall socket, you're putting your Mac at the mercy of the power company, your home's wiring, and all the things that can go wrong in between: brownouts, voltage spikes, lightning, you name it. Your Mac's power supply is pretty robust, but a single random power surge can still fry its circuits. Even when the electricity appears to be flowing correctly, imperceptible fluctuations in the current can cause computer components to deteriorate more quickly than normal.

So please, take the basic precaution of using a surge protector. They come in many shapes, sizes, and prices—some with every bell and whistle, and some quite plain. Not all work equally well, so look for a model with a good warranty that covers not only the protector itself but also the equipment attached to it, in the event of a surge.

Better yet, consider buying a small UPS (uninterruptible power supply). A UPS contains a battery with enough juice to power your computer for anywhere from a few minutes to a few hours, along with circuitry to convert the battery's DC output to AC and switch over to the battery instantly and seamlessly in the event of a power outage. If the power goes out for more than a very brief period, the UPS sounds an alarm so that you will know to save your work and shut down your computer safely before the battery goes out. (Some UPS units include software to handle automated shutdowns.) In addition to protecting your computer from power outages, a UPS conditions the electricity flowing through it and absorbs surges.

A Conversation about Surge Protectors and UPSes

Do you really need a surge protector? Is a UPS worth the extra money? The experts weigh in:

Sharon Zardetto Aker: In 20 years of having multiple Macs (there are a half dozen in use in the house right now), 10 years of which was in the country where power came and went with strong breezes, I've never had a surge problem affect any Mac, nor do I know of anyone who has ever had that problem, so I'm a little uncomfortable with this recommendation.

Dan Frakes: Consider yourself lucky! In my humble opinion, no computer should ever be run without a surge protector. All it takes is one incident to make a believer out of you!

Kirk McElhearn: I agree with Dan.

Adam Engst: Personally, I never use surge protectors, but I wouldn't run a Mac without a UPS. Power flickers too often for my taste, and preventing the lost work is worth it.

Tonya Engst: I've found that an important side effect of running a UPS, in addition to allowing a graceful shutdown at the beginning of a power outage, is that I can work on days when the power flickers frequently. In Seattle, probably once a month or more, and here in Ithaca, certainly once every 6 weeks, the power goes out maybe 8 times, for about 20 seconds each time, over the course of an afternoon. Without the UPS, I wouldn't be able to work effectively on those days.

Geoff Duncan: I feel more comfortable recommending a voltage regulator or a power conditioner instead of consumer-level surge protectors, which are usually pretty useless. UPSes are even better.

My favorite UPS manufacturer is APC (American Power Conversion). To find one of their models that suits your needs, use their product selector at `www.apcc.com/template/size/apc/`. Other UPS manufacturers that offer Mac-compatible software include:

- Belkin (`http://catalog.belkin.com/IWCatSectionView.process?IWAction=Load&Section_Id=76`)

- MGE UPS Systems (`www.mgeups.com/selector/ups/index.php`)

- Xantrex (`www.preparedwithpower.com/backup/`)

Perform Daily Tasks

If you performed all the preliminary steps in Chapter 1, your daily maintenance ritual consists of at most two tasks, and at best, none!

Back Up Changed Files

In the type of backup system I recommend (see Chapter 9 for complete details), your backup software begins by copying all your important files to some sort of external media—preferably a hard drive. What counts as "important" is up to you; it could be everything on your disk, just the contents of your home folder or your Documents folder, or just the files you're actively working on. But at a minimum, you should make a daily copy of any files you could not re-create in a matter of minutes, such as your saved email, photographs, and any documents you've spent hours working on during the day.

I advocate performing *additive incremental archives*. This means that after your first full backup of all the files you want (creating the *archive*), each successive daily backup copies only those files that are new, or have changed, since the last time (that's the *incremental* part); and it keeps the previous copies of your files, so you can go back to an earlier version if you accidentally modify a file you shouldn't have (that's the *additive* part; it also means that files you delete on your hard disk remain in the archive).

Note: In addition to automated daily backups, it never hurts to make extra copies of files you're actively working on. If you take a moment to drag such files to a network server or iDisk (or even make an extra copy on the same drive) whenever you stop to take a break, you'll add yet another layer of safety to your valuable data.

If you configured your backup software to run on a schedule, this happens automatically every day. You may, however, need to intervene in some cases, such as these:

♦ If you back up to optical discs, in which case you must insert new media as requested

♦ If you back up to a server that requires you to log in manually

♦ If you back up from, or to, a computer that's not always available at the same time of day (such as an iBook, PowerBook, or MacBook Pro)

Even if your backup software runs automatically, I recommend checking its logs regularly to make sure that it ran and that it backed up all the files you expected it to.

Download Software Updates

Earlier, I suggested setting Software Update to check for, and download, any new updates from Apple daily. If you followed that advice, any important updates download in the background, and Software Update informs you when they're ready to install. So your daily task is more of a *don't* than a *do:* on the days when that inevitable alert appears, asking if you want to install the latest software updates, read about the updates but consider postponing installation for a few days—in other words, click Quit instead of Install.

I say this for two reasons. First, software updates take some time to download and install, and you may not have the time available at the instant Software Update informs you that new software is ready. Besides, updates occasionally result in a cascading effect: now that you've updated X, Y no longer works and must be updated; now that Y has been updated, you must make changes to Z's settings. For this reason, I find Saturday mornings especially good for updating software.

Second, in the unlikely event that an update contains a major error—as has happened a few times—waiting gives you a safety buffer. If you check sites like MacInTouch (`www.macintouch.com`) or MacFixIt (`www.macfixit.com`), you can get a sense of whether an update has raised any serious issues for other Macintosh users. However, take isolated reports of problems

---

A Conversation about Software Updates

Many people install software updates as soon as they appear, but I recommend doing it once a week instead. Here's what some other experts have to say on the subject:

Kirk McElhearn: Daily isn't always best for updates—it means you're on the cutting edge and, since we've seen a handful of Apple updates that were pulled or quickly revised in recent years, it might be more risky than it's worth.

Andy Affleck: I agree with Kirk; daily software updates are very risky. I generally check MacFixIt and MacInTouch for a few days after each update to be sure it's a safe one. Doing software updates weekly is safer.

Tonya Engst: I usually run Apple's Software Update utility during the weekend, because if an update involves restarting it's too much time out of the day, plus it's a distraction from getting my work done.

Chris Pepper: In my department, we have the "Never on Friday" rule. The gist is that you should (a) assume that any work might go horribly pear-shaped, and (b) never start a process you're not prepared to see through to its conclusion. Since we don't like staying late Friday night or working Saturday, we don't start major upgrades on Friday afternoon (unless they're scheduled to run through the weekend). For any substantial maintenance

(weekly, monthly, and especially annual), it's probably worth running or checking a backup first, and making sure you have twice as much time as you expect to need, so you don't start a process on Friday afternoon and suck away your weekend if the upgrade doesn't go smoothly.

Geoff Duncan: I check on Mondays but usually don't install anything at that point. Security updates have highest priority with me; I might apply them as early as Wednesday. Anything else has to wait until immediately after a backup and, following Chris's postulate that it's going to take at least twice as long as I think it will, until I have time.

with a grain of salt. Updates can fail—or appear to fail—for many reasons, including user error. The fact that one or two people cry wolf should not dissuade you from applying an update.

Perform Weekly Tasks

Your daily maintenance tasks are minor—and perhaps they even happen automatically. Once a week, however, you should set aside time for some more in-depth housekeeping. Depending on your work habits and system specifications, these weekly tasks might take 15 minutes or they might take a couple of hours. If you find that you can't finish them all conveniently in one sitting, feel free to stagger them—one each day of the week, for example—as long as any given task occurs about once every week.

Clean Up Your Desktop

I want to ask you a personal question. How many icons—not counting hard disks, network volumes, and removable media—are sitting on your Desktop right now? (My answer: 11, though I usually try to keep it closer to 6. Ask me again tomorrow, after I've performed my weekly housekeeping.) I know lots of people who regularly have dozens or even hundreds of icons on their Desktops, who use it as a catchall for downloaded files, work in progress, email enclosures, and everything else that needs a temporary home. This is a bad idea! Here's why:

- Mac OS X considers every icon on your Desktop a window, and because every open window uses up a certain amount of RAM, more Desktop icons means greater RAM usage.

- Exposé shortcuts notwithstanding, putting files and folders on your Desktop makes them harder to find, because they're so easily hidden behind windows. (You can, of course, access the contents of your Desktop folder in a regular Finder window, but some people put items on the Desktop specifically to avoid working with Finder windows.)

- Your Desktop displays files and folders in icon view, unlike the more efficient list and column views available in other windows. (Yes, I know, you can view the contents of your Desktop folder in a window too, but work with me here…)

- Tossing lots of files into a single big storage area (wherever it may be) creates more work later on when you try to locate specific files.

- If you use your Desktop to hold important items that you want to keep "in your face" at all times, you'll lose that effect when the files become too numerous.

A cluttered Desktop slows you down, so take a few minutes once a week to organize most (if not all) the items on your Desktop into other folders.

I know of numerous organizational philosophies, but I have no wish to impose a rigid system on you. Instead, simply consider these suggestions for keeping files off your Desktop:

- If your chief concern is keeping track of a few important files, use the Finder's label feature (select a file and choose a color label from the bottom of the Edit menu) to mark all high-priority files in a given color. Then, use a smart folder to display all files on your disk labeled with that color. Choose File > New Smart Folder, choose Color Label from the first pop-up menu, and click the color you used to label the files. Then click Save and give your smart folder a name. The folder automatically updates itself to display all the files labeled with the selected color, wherever they may be stored on your disk.

Tip: For details on using smart folders, you can read an article I wrote for *Macworld* magazine titled "Cut through the Clutter" (www.macworld.com/2006/01/secrets/febworkingmac/).

♦ If you store downloaded files on your Desktop, instead make a new folder named Downloads, put *that* on your Desktop (or somewhere else convenient, such as in your Documents folder), and keep the downloaded files inside it.

Tip: To change the location to which Safari downloads files, choose Safari > Preferences, click the General button, and choose a location from the Save Downloaded Files To pop-up menu (choose Other to select any folder on your disk).

♦ Check your Desktop for files you no longer need, such as software you've already installed, PDFs you downloaded and printed, or out-dated text clippings, and delete them.

♦ Several Mac OS X applications function as excellent snippet keepers, giving you a much better place to store things that might otherwise go on your Desktop (URLs, saved Web pages, text clippings, PDF and text files, and so on). Examples include:

   ♦ **DEVONthink** (http://devon-technologies.com/; Personal edition, $40, or Professional edition, $75)

   ♦ **NoteBook** (www.circusponies.com; $50)

   ♦ **SOHO Notes**, shown in **Figure 5** (www.chronosnet.com; $70)

   ♦ **Yojimbo** (www.barebones.com; $40)

Figure 5

SOHO Notes is a competent all-purpose snippet keeper.

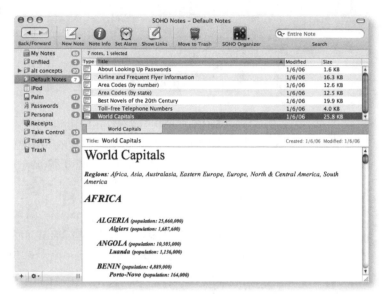

One way or another, try to get your total number of Desktop icons below a dozen or so. You'll be surprised how much this simple step improves your efficiency.

Tip: If you keep files and folders on your Desktop because you find it difficult to work with Finder windows, you may be able to improve your experience considerably by customizing the default Finder window. You can learn about Finder customization in Matt Neuburg's *Take Control of Customizing Tiger* (www.takecontrolbooks.com/tiger-customizing.html).

Back Up Everything

You already back up important changed files every day to an archive, but a thorough backup plan also includes a bootable duplicate of your entire hard disk, which enables you to recover almost instantly from even a complete drive failure, with all your files intact. You can certainly update this duplicate every day if you wish, but because the process typically takes longer than updating an archive, I suggest updating your duplicate at least once a week.

If you configured your backup software to run on a schedule, your duplicate should update itself automatically every week. If you opted for manual duplicates (or if the drive you use for duplicates isn't always connected), update your duplicate now.

Note: Most backup software, when duplicating your drive onto an external volume, automatically performs an incremental backup—copying only those files that are new or changed since your last duplicate, and deleting files from the external volume that are no longer on your internal disk.

Rotate Backups Offsite

I recommended maintaining at least two sets of backup media—for example, two hard drives, each with a partition for a duplicate and another to hold your archives. With two copies of your backups, you can keep one next to your computer, ready for the next day's backup, and another in a safe place offsite. That way, if disaster strikes your home or office and takes out one of your backups, you have another to fall back on. If you swap your backup sets weekly, you'll rest secure knowing that even in the worst possible case, you'll lose no more than one week's data.

Today, after your backup software updates your daily archive and weekly duplicate, make the switch. Take the most recently used media and move it to another building, such as a friend's house or your office (if your computer is at home). Then, bring back the media you stored there last week, and you'll be ready for a new round of backups. You might even agree to a swap arrangement with a friend: every week you trade hard drives, giving each of you an offsite location for your data while keeping it in trusted hands.

Use Software Update to Install Apple Software Updates

Software Update checks for new versions of any Apple software you have installed and (if you set it to do so) downloads them automatically. However, as I mentioned in *Download Software Updates* (page 34), you may wish to hold off on installing the downloaded updates until you have more free time and have checked to make sure they contain no serious flaws. When you're ready to install the updates, follow these steps:

1. Choose Software Update from the Apple menu. Software Update checks for updates and displays a list of any it finds, including those it has already downloaded but not yet installed (**Figure 6**). (If no updates are available, Software Update displays a message that says "Your software is up to date." Click OK, and skip the rest of these steps.)

Figure 6

Select software updates to install in this window.

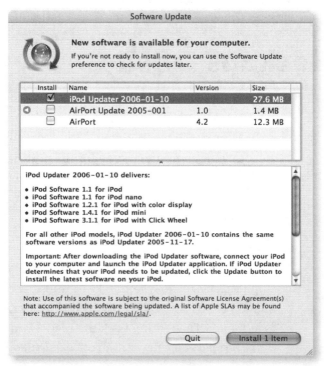

2. Check the boxes in the Install column for the items you want to install. (Items with a ⬤ icon require a restart after installation.)

3. Some items may not apply to you. For example, if you don't have an iPod, AirPort base station, or iSight camera, you can skip software updates for these items. In such cases, you can prevent Software Update from listing an item the next time it opens by selecting the item and clicking Delete. (If you later wish to see items you removed in this way, choose Software Update > Reset Ignored Updates.)

4. Click Install, and click through any license agreements that appear.

Software Update installs your new software, prompting you to restart if necessary. If no restart is necessary, click Quit.

Check for Third-Party Software Updates

Like Apple's Software Update, third-party applications that have built-in automatic update checkers give you the option of postponing an update until a more convenient time. But some applications check only when you explicitly tell them to. Therefore, take a few minutes to launch your most frequently used applications and use their Check for Updates features. Download and install any free updates now, following the developers' instructions.

Tip: Another way to check for the latest software is to subscribe to VersionTracker Pro. This service includes software that runs on your Mac and alerts you when updates to any of your installed software become available, at which time you can download and install them with a couple of clicks. VersionTracker Pro monitors up to three Macs for an annual fee of $50 (www.versiontracker.com/subscribe/mactrial/).

Reboot If Performance Seems Slow

Some people turn off their Macs whenever they aren't in use, either to save electricity or simply out of habit. Others leave them on all the time, on the basis that sleep mode uses a trivially small amount of energy and enables you to get back to work more quickly. (I fall into the latter group, turning off my Macs only when I go on vacation, or when for some other reason I expect to be away from them for more than a day.)

If you leave your Mac on all the time, you may find that over a period of days or weeks, its performance slowly degrades. One common reason for this phenomenon is memory leaks (see *RAM Usage,* page 76), but other kinds of bugs can also lead to excessive RAM and CPU usage that gradually bogs down your system. In addition, as you use your Mac it may create virtual memory swap files on your hard disk if you run low on physical RAM; the more of these files actively in use, the slower your computer runs.

When you begin to notice that your Mac doesn't feel as peppy as usual, try restarting (by choosing Restart from the Apple menu). If you use lots of resource-intensive applications and have a slower machine with comparatively little RAM, you may need to restart as frequently as every day; if you never notice any slowdowns, once a month may be adequate. You be the judge.

I talk more about keeping an eye on potential performance problems later, in Chapter 8.

Consider Clearing Certain Caches

As you use various applications, they often store frequently used information in files called *caches.* For example, when you visit a Web site in Safari, it stores the images from that site in a cache, so that the next time you go to the site, it can display the images more quickly (because it doesn't have to download them again). Another example is Microsoft Word, which can display the fonts in the Fonts menu in their own typefaces. If Word had to read in all those fonts each time you used it in order to build the Font menu, every launch could take a minute or more, so Word builds a cache that contains all the data it needs to draw the font names.

Caches are good things—usually. Sometimes they cause more problems than they solve. One problem occurs when an application has cached hundreds or thousands of files—so many that reading in the caches takes longer than reading (or recomputing) the data they contain, thus slowing down the application instead of speeding it up! A more serious problem involves damaged cache files. Maybe an application failed to write the file correctly in the first place, maybe the information it put into the cache was bad, or maybe a disk error corrupted the cache after the fact. Whatever the reason, a corrupted cache file can cause an application to crash, run slowly, or exhibit any number of incorrect behaviors.

Note: I discuss caches in some detail in a *Macworld* magazine article titled "34 Software Speedups" (`www.macworld.com/2006/02/features/softwarespeed/`).

Several utilities provide a one-click method for deleting one or all of your caches. I recommend against blindly deleting all your caches; as I said, they *usually* help rather than hinder. However, a few caches in particular have notorious reputations, and clearing them periodically tends to make the applications that use them run more smoothly. My recommendations for weekly cache maintenance are as follows:

♦ Clear your Safari cache by choosing Safari > Empty Cache (Command-Option-E).

Tip: Alternatively, you can disable Safari's cache altogether. In the Finder, navigate to the folder `~/Library/Caches/Safari`. Select this folder and choose File > Get Info. In the Ownership & Permissions section of the Info window, choose Read Only from the pop-up menu, and then close the Info window. This prevents Safari from being able to write new files into the cache folder.

♦ Safari stores *favicons* (those tiny icons that appear next to a site's URL in the address bar) separately from the main cache. To remove them, quit Safari and drag the folder `~/Library/Safari/Icons` to the Trash.

♦ Mac OS X maintains a system-level font cache that numerous applications use. Bad font cache files have been implicated in numerous problems. The easiest way to wipe out these caches is by using Font Finagler (`http://homepage.mac.com/mdouma46/fontfinagler/`; $10), shown in **Figure 7**. Or, to delete most of your font caches manually, drag the folder `/Library/Caches/com.Apple.ATS` to the Trash. Enter your password when prompted to do so, and click OK. Then restart your computer and empty your Trash.

Figure 7

Font Finagler's Font Cache Cleaner window lists all your system's font caches and lets you delete them with a single click.

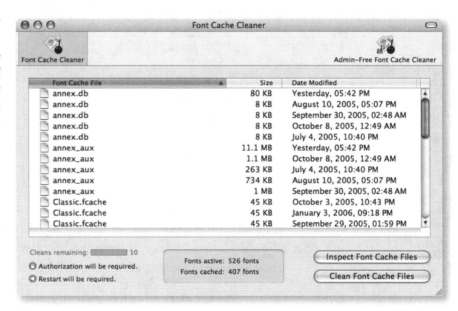

♦ Microsoft Office's font cache seems more prone to problems than the systemwide font cache. To clear it, quit all your Office applications and then drag the file `~/Library/Preferences/Microsoft/Office Font Cache (11)` to the Trash.

Perform Monthly Tasks

Once a month—perhaps on a different day from the one on which you perform your weekly tasks—set aside about 15 minutes to perform four additional maintenance tasks: emptying your trash, running Disk Utility, cleaning your screen, and cleaning your mouse or trackball.

Empty Your Trash

I have no doubt that some readers are now concluding I'm out of my mind. *Empty my Trash once a month?! What could he be thinking?* The thing is, of those people, some of them are thinking that once a month is far too seldom, and others are thinking it's far too often!

Your Trash, as you probably know, is simply another folder. As a result, moving files or folders to the Trash does not delete them, just as tossing a crumpled paper in a physical trash can doesn't automatically turn it into landfill. On your Mac, as in your home, the contents of the Trash continue to take up space until you empty the Trash (in the Finder, choose File > Empty Trash). When you empty the Trash, you free up that now-unused space for other files.

How often should you do this? It depends on how you think about the Trash.

Let me put my cards on the table: I am a compulsive Trash emptier. I picked up this habit many years ago when I was struggling to make do with a 20 MB hard disk and every kilobyte counted. If I left items in the Trash without emptying it for more than a few hours, I'd run out of space—simple as that. Today, even though I have a large hard drive with plenty of free space, I still haven't kicked that habit. On the other hand, because I know I'll be emptying the Trash shortly after putting a file there, I tend to think of moving files to the Trash as a final deletion from which recovery is impossible, so I don't take that step unless I'm entirely sure I can do without that file.

On the other end of the spectrum are what I'll call pack rats. They cringe at the idea of getting rid of anything for good. For them, the Trash is just another folder, and unlike a physical trash can, it never gets full. You can keep putting stuff in there for as long as you want. So they freely move files and folders to the Trash that don't seem especially important at the moment—just to get them out of the way—because they realize they can open up that folder at any time and get the files back.

In between, of course, are most of the rest of us. Each person's Trash philosophy is a bit different from the next person's. If you're that hypothetical person right in the middle of the Trash emptying spectrum—neither a pack rat nor a compulsive emptier—let's just say that today is a good day to empty the Trash.

For everyone else, here are some reasons why you might want to move toward the center, toward what I'm proposing as the happy medium of monthly Trash emptying.

For those on the compulsive side, consider this:

♦ Everyone makes mistakes. You can probably recall at least one occasion when you had to fish a file out of the Trash. Remember that once you've emptied the Trash, the only way to recover deleted files is to try expensive (and often unsuccessful) undelete utilities or to send your drive to a much more expensive data recovery service. Giving yourself a bit of a safety net might save you grief later.

♦ Modern hard drives are large enough that you probably won't run out of space if you wait a few weeks before emptying the Trash.

♦ You'll be able to focus on your work and be more productive if you don't keep glancing down to see if the Trash can is full.

For those who lean more toward being pack rats, think about this:

♦ How many times have you had to recover a file from the Trash that was more than a month old? Ever? If that's a common occurrence, you should seriously consider revising your filing habits.

♦ Hard drives are large, but not infinite. You will eventually run out of space. In the meantime, all those extra files can contribute to increased file fragmentation, potentially decreasing your Mac's performance.

♦ All those extra files, merely by sitting in the Trash, could result in productivity losses due to misleading Spotlight searches and longer waits for backups and diagnostic utilities to run.

A Conversation about Emptying the Trash

How often should you empty your Trash? Let's ask the experts:

Sharon Zardetto Aker: I've always recommended, especially to the pack rats, that they create a folder called "To the Trash" and put stuff in there. At intervals, sort by modified date and anything older than [choose the age] goes to the Trash and gets emptied. You lose the convenience of having Command-Delete send to the Trash this way, but you don't have to review the Trash contents.

Kirk McElhearn: One problem with that approach is like-named files that overwrite existing files in the "To the Trash" folder. This doesn't happen with the Trash, which renames files if necessary.

Peter N Lewis: I'm not a pack rat, but I've trained myself to never empty the Trash unless absolutely needed. I find it hard to believe that issues of fragmentation and what-have-you are going to slow the computer down noticeably if you have a large hard drive that never comes near being full. Backups can be configured to avoid backing up the Trash folder if necessary.

Adam Engst: I'm with Peter on this; I empty the Trash only when I need the disk space or when there's some other reason to eliminate a particular file entirely (and when I'm too lazy to get rid of it individually via Terminal).

Joe Kissell: One big advantage to frequent Trash emptying is that Spotlight searches don't produce long lists of deleted (and therefore, in my way of working at least, irrelevant) files.

Tonya Engst: So many of the files in my Trash begin with "TCo" (for *Take Control of*) that I like to clear it out periodically so that I can easily find stuff if I put it in there accidentally. Otherwise, I'm scrolling through hundreds of versions of old manuscripts.

And for everyone, regardless of how frequently you decide to empty the Trash, here's one huge piece of advice: look before you leap. Get into the habit of opening the Trash folder (by clicking the Trash icon in your Dock) and scanning its contents before you empty it. It may take you a few minutes, but you're far less likely to delete a file by mistake that way.

Use Disk Utility's Repair Disk Feature

Earlier, I suggested using Disk Utility's Repair Disk feature to preemptively check for and eliminate common disk gremlins (see *Run Disk Utility*, page 25). Because disk errors do creep in during ordinary computer use (seemingly of their own accord), I suggest running Disk Utility and using its Repair Disk command once a month.

Why Do Disk Errors Occur?

In addition to Disk Utility, numerous third-party utilities check for, and attempt to repair, a wide range of disk errors. I've run these utilities hundreds of times over the years, and a shockingly large proportion of the time they've found and fixed errors—even though I wasn't aware of any problem. What causes these problems in the first place?

Although I can't give you a complete answer to this question, I can offer a few reasons *some* disk errors occur:

Buggy software: Virtually all software contains some bugs, and bugs can cause bad data to be written to your disk or can corrupt existing data.

Hardware failures: If your hard drive, logic board, or various other components have manufacturing defects—or develop malfunctions later on—these can result in disk errors.

User error: If you unplug an external hard drive without unmounting the volume(s) first (File > Eject), you may interrupt the flow of data to the drive, or interrupt a housekeeping procedure. Many other user errors can also result in disk problems.

Power failure: If the power goes out (or your battery dies) at an inopportune moment, a file may not be written properly.

In other words, stuff happens. You can guard against some problems simply by being careful, but stuff will still happen.

Clean Your Screen

Your computer's display attracts dust, and over time that can impair the screen's readability. (It's also, let's face it, just yucky.) Once a month, or whenever you can see a thin layer of dust on a black screen, give it a quick cleaning.

To clean a screen, use a soft, lint-free cloth—not a paper towel—moistened slightly with water to prevent static buildup. You can also use cleaning solutions designed expressly for computer displays—I've had good results with iKlear screen cleaning products from Klear Screen (`www.klearscreen.com`)—but avoid anything containing alcohol or ammonia. Wipe the screen gently; LCD displays, especially, can be damaged by excessive force.

Clean Your Mouse or Trackball

I spent five years working for Kensington, a company that made its reputation in the Mac world by selling fantastic mice and trackballs. During the time I worked there, we saw the computing world transition from opto-mechanical devices (in which a ball turns slotted rollers connected to wheels whose speed and direction were measured with photosensors) to purely optical devices (in which a tiny camera tracks changes in the texture of your desk's surface, or the trackball's surface).

The biggest and most exciting advantage of optical designs was supposed to be that they never had to be cleaned. Gone were the old days of disassembling a mouse, losing the ball as it rolls across your office floor, and fumbling with cotton swabs to clean dirt and hair off of tiny rollers—a procedure you might have to repeat every few weeks or so. Optical mice have no moving parts—no rollers, no ball—so cleaning should never be necessary.

Experience has shown that although optical devices require *less* cleaning, they still require *some*. Specifically, optical mice tend to accumulate dust inside the opening at the bottom (often shaped like a keyhole) through which the sensor watches your desktop. If it becomes clogged, your pointer may move erratically, or not at all.

Optical trackballs have a similar opening above the lens (remove the trackball from the casing to see it) with a similar tendency to attract dust. In addition, the tiny bearings or rollers on which the ball rests can collect dust and hair, preventing the ball from moving smoothly.

And, of course, plenty of Mac users still have older pointing devices that use the ball-and-roller mechanisms and therefore require what we now think of as old-fashioned cleaning.

Your input device most likely came with cleaning instructions, so I'll simply say: follow them now. If you don't have the instructions (and can't find them on the manufacturer's Web site), they generally boil down to removing visible dust and gunk from wheels, rollers, bearings, and other moving parts (and away from the openings used by optical sensors). A slightly moistened cotton swab will do the job nicely.

Tip: Cleaning Mighty Mouse's Scroll Ball. The miniature trackball that enables you to scroll with an Apple Mighty Mouse can accumulate dirt, leading to poor scrolling performance. You can't remove the ball, but you can generally dislodge any dirt by inverting the mouse, pressing the ball inward as far as it will go (it springs inward slightly), and rolling it vigorously in every direction. If scrolling is still not smooth after you do this, repeat the procedure using a slightly moistened cloth or paper towel.

For most people, once a month is a reasonable cleaning interval. If you have pets, you may need to clean your mouse or trackball more frequently; if you work in an Intel clean room, maybe never!

Exercise Your Notebook's Battery

Early portable computers used NiCad batteries, which were subject to the dreaded "memory" effect. To get maximum run time from them, you had to discharge them completely before recharging them; if you failed to do this, even a fully charged battery might suddenly run out of power after a short time.

The lithium-ion batteries used in modern Mac notebooks (and iPods) don't suffer from memory, but according to Apple they still need to be "exercised" (that is, discharged and recharged periodically) for maximum performance. If you leave your notebook plugged in all the time, the battery never discharges beyond a few percentage points, so it gets insufficient exercise. For such users, Apple recommends that once a month you unplug your computer, run it on the battery until it discharges completely, and then recharge it.

For more information about Apple's notebook batteries, check out www.apple.com/batteries/.

Perform Yearly Tasks

If you've ever looked around your home and thought, "It's time for a good spring cleaning," you know the value of decluttering. On your computer, as in your home, make an annual ritual of removing dirt, tossing out junk, and putting your belongings in order. Besides giving you a cleaner, more inviting environment, these yearly tasks can extend your computer's life span and help keep your data safe.

De-Dust Your Mac

Nearly all Mac models employ one or more internal cooling fans. Without them, your computer would overheat, leading to crashes, erratic behavior, and possibly even permanent damage to sensitive components.

But as the fans pull air into the computer, they also pull in dust. Dust can accumulate on the air intake vents, on the fan itself, or on any surface along the flow of air within the computer. When a layer of dust sits atop a hot component, it acts as an insulator, preventing some of the heat from escaping into the air. And if dust blocks the air flow, the heat that does escape has nowhere to go. Either way, your fan must work harder, which not only makes it noisier but also makes it suck in even more dust.

In short, dust is no friend of computers. By the simple act of getting rid of the dust, you can make your Mac cooler and quieter—and prevent all sorts of unpleasant problems.

You can remove dust by brushing or wiping, by vacuuming, or by blowing it off with compressed air. The compressed-air approach is the least desirable, because it puts the dust right back into the air. I prefer an ordinary vacuum cleaner with a hose attachment, but before using such a vacuum on the *inside* of your computer, take note of the warning just ahead. If you choose the brushing or wiping approach, be sure to use a *soft, dry* cloth or a *soft, dry* brush—and a gentle touch.

Warning! *Conventional AC-powered vacuum cleaners, particularly those with plastic nozzles, can in theory build up enough static charge to damage your computer's circuitry if used on the inside of a case. For vacuuming the inside of a computer, use either a battery-powered vacuum or an antistatic vacuum designed expressly for cleaning electronic equipment. In any case, be careful not to touch the nozzle to any components inside your computer.*

To de-dust your Mac, follow these steps:

1. Shut down and unplug your computer; also unplug any peripherals or other cables.

2. Be sure you have room to work in. If your computer is located under a desk, for instance, move it out into the open.

3. Using your dust-removal tool of choice, remove dust from in or around any holes or slots on the outside of the case. Be aware that some of these openings may be on the bottom or the back of the case, depending on the design.

These remaining steps are for desktop computers only:

4. Following the instructions that came with your computer for installing RAM or other internal options, carefully open the case. The method for doing this varies widely from model to model. For example:

- Most Power Mac models have a side panel that you can remove without tools by opening a latch.

- Remove the back cover of iMac G5 models by placing the computer face down on a soft cloth and loosening three screws in the grill on the bottom.

- For iMac G4 models, turn the computer on its side (again, using a soft cloth to protect the display), and loosen the screws on the bottom plate.

Note: Some iBook and PowerBook models have removable keyboards or other ways to access the innards without performing major surgery. But even if you can see part of the computer's insides, you're unlikely to be able to reach spots where dust might accumulate. My advice is to leave the inside of a portable Mac alone; if you have reason to believe you have an internal dust problem, find an authorized service technician to open up the computer and clean it for you.

---

5. Once again, remove any visible dust using your tool of choice. If your Power Mac has add-in PCI or video cards, be sure to remove the dust from them as well. (In some cases, you may need to remove the card from the computer, de-dust, and reinsert it. If you do remove a PCI card, be sure to ground yourself—ideally, by wearing an antistatic strap—while handling it.)

Warning! Be extremely careful when removing dust from the inside of your computer! If using a vacuum cleaner, avoid touching the hose tip or brush to any surface. If using a brush or cloth, apply the gentlest pressure possible.

6. Close the computer's case, reattach peripherals and other cables, and turn it back on.

Warning! Avoid the temptation to perform any further disassembly on your computer beyond merely opening the case. As a general rule, if you have trouble reaching some spot inside your computer, so does dust.

Clean Your Keyboard

Before you put away that vacuum cleaner or canned air, give your keyboard a once-over too, following these steps:

1. Unplug the keyboard from your computer. (For portables, turn off the computer.)

2. Most keyboards cannot be disassembled easily, so don't even try. Instead, simply invert and shake to dislodge any large particles. For larger or more stubborn particles, you may need to use tweezers or a slightly moistened cotton swab.

3. Run the vacuum cleaner or compressed air between all rows of keys.

4. Using a soft and *very slightly* damp cloth, carefully wipe the keycaps clean. (Some heavy-duty stains may require the use of a mild all-purpose cleaner, but be sparing, because fluid that drips into the keyboard circuitry can damage it.)

5. If you're the patient type and your keyboard is especially cruddy, use a *very slightly* moistened cotton swab to clean the sides of the keys.

6. Plug your keyboard back in.

Clean Your iSight

If your computer has an iSight camera (either built in or external), this is also a good time to make sure it can see you clearly. Follow these steps:

1. Unplug your iSight (if appropriate).

2. Use a soft, *very slightly* damp cloth (or lens-cleaning paper, available from any camera store) to wipe the front surface, applying only gentle pressure.

   Warning! *Do not use alcohol, ammonia, or any other chemicals; use only water.*

3. Buff with a soft, dry cloth.

Make Archival Backups to DVD

By now, regular backups are a normal part of your routine: your backup software automatically updates your archives every day and your duplicates once a week, and you diligently rotate backup media offsite—right? Even so, I recommend adding one final element to your backup regimen: archival DVDs.

If you've followed my advice, you already have archives of all your important files—going back several months or more—on each of two or more hard drives. You also have one or more complete, bootable copies of your main hard disk as it existed at some recent time. This is all good, but some problems remain:

+ Hard drives don't last forever. Sooner or later—in a year, or five or ten years—you'll no longer be able to access the data on your drives.

+ Because archives constantly get bigger, the archive can eventually outgrow the drive you store it on.

+ As your main hard disk fills up, you may want to delete files periodically to save space and yet be able to retrieve those old files if you later need them.

I'm aware of several schools of thought regarding archival backups, so bear in mind that this is just one person's take on the process. In a nutshell, I recommend this: once a year, make a copy of all your backups (both archive and duplicate) onto a stack of DVDs, store them in a safe place, and then recycle the hard disk you use for archives by erasing it and starting over with a new, full backup. By doing this, you hedge your bets against hard drive failure, free up valuable space for archives, and give yourself a safety net in case you want to prune files on your primary hard disk.

Note: I hasten to point out that DVDs don't last forever either, but if you store them carefully in a dark, cool, dry place, they should be readable for ten years. By the time you approach that point, if you still want to keep the data, you should migrate the contents of your discs onto new media.

To archive your data, obtain a big stack of recordable DVDs and follow these steps:

1. Make sure you have a backup application that can create duplicates and span data across multiple discs. (See Appendix B for suggestions.)

2. Attach the drive you use for archives (if it's not already attached).

3. Following the instructions included with your backup application, select your archive drive as the source and your DVD burner as the destination.

4. Begin the backup process, feeding in blank discs as needed.

5. When the backup completes, repeat Steps 3 and 4 with your primary hard disk as the source (or, if you prefer, use a recent duplicate as the source).

6. Store your newly burned DVDs in a dark, cool, dry place.

    Better yet, if you can afford the time and the media—make *two* complete copies of both archives and duplicates, and store them in different places.

7. Configure your backup software to replace the existing archive with a fresh, full backup on its next run. (In some cases, you may need to erase the drive manually first.) Again, consult the documentation that came with your backup software for details.

Now that you have a safe copy of all your data, you can consider deleting files to make extra space on your main hard drive, as I describe in the following section.

Remove Unneeded Files

Just as your home probably needs a good spring cleaning once a year, your computer can use a digital tidying-up now and then. So take this opportunity to get rid of applications you don't use, outdated files you'll never look at again, and any other crud that has gathered in the dark corners of your hard disk.

The process is the same one I described near the beginning of this book. Flip back to *Clean Out Accumulated Cruft* (page 16) for complete instructions, and repeat that procedure now.

Change Your Passwords

Passwords are a fact of life in the wired 21st century. You probably have dozens or even hundreds of passwords, such as these:

◆ Your Mac OS X administrator password

◆ Passwords for .Mac and any other email accounts you may have

◆ Passwords for Web sites and other online services

◆ A password for your AirPort base station, and perhaps another one for your wireless network

◆ Passwords that protect encrypted files, folders, or volumes (such as your backups)

It's easy to become lazy—choosing short, easy-to-type (and easy-to-remember) passwords and reusing the same password in multiple places. The Mac OS X keychain enables you to store most of your passwords in one place and access them easily, but it can also contribute to password laziness by keeping you from noticing how often your passwords are required.

If you're the only person who uses your computer, and if you don't access sensitive information online (such as bank accounts or proprietary corporate data), you can probably get away with relatively few passwords that remain the same indefinitely. Otherwise, I strongly recommend changing your passwords—at least, those that protect the most sensitive information—once a year (or more often). That way, if someone were to guess one of your passwords, it would be useful for only a limited period of time.

Look for Passwords to Change

Each Web site, application, or device has its own procedure for changing passwords, and I can't begin to cover them all here. I will, however, mention a few common places to look:

♦ To change your Mac OS X user account password, go to the Accounts pane of System Preferences. Select your user name in the list on the left and click the Change Password button in the Password view.

♦ To change your .Mac password, go to `www.mac.com` and click the Log In link on the right side of the blue .Mac tab, which runs across the top of the window just under the row of tabs. Enter your member name and password. Then click your member name on the .Mac tab (logging in again if asked to do so) to display the Account Settings page, click Password Settings, and follow the instructions.

♦ To change the password used by your AirPort base station or your wireless network, open AirPort Admin Utility (in `/Applications/Utilities`). Select your base station and click Configure. Then, in the AirPort view, to change the password of the base station itself, click Change Password. To change the password of your wireless network, click Change Wireless Security.

In addition, I recommend opening Keychain Access (which is also in `/Applications/Utilities`) and looking through the passwords stored there. That will give you an important reminder of many of the Web sites and applications for which you've already established passwords.

Choose a Good Password

You've undoubtedly heard this sermon before, so I won't beat you over the head with it, but let me briefly reiterate the qualities of a good password:

◆ **Longer is better:** A 16-character password is much more secure than a 6-character password, and even longer is better still.

◆ **No common words:** Don't use a word (or words) from the dictionary as your password; a hacker can break it easily. Also avoid words and numbers people might guess: your favorite color, date of birth, pet's name, and so on.

◆ **Mix letters, case, and numerals:** Every password should include at least one uppercase letter, at least one lowercase letter, and at least one numeral.

Luckily, Tiger includes a tool to help you create passwords that meet these requirements: Password Assistant. Whenever you create a new password (for instance, in the Keychain Access utility or in the Accounts pane of System Preferences), a 🔑 button appears next to the New Password field. Click this button to display Password Assistant (**Figure 8**).

Figure 8

Password Assistant enables you to generate passwords of any desired length and type.

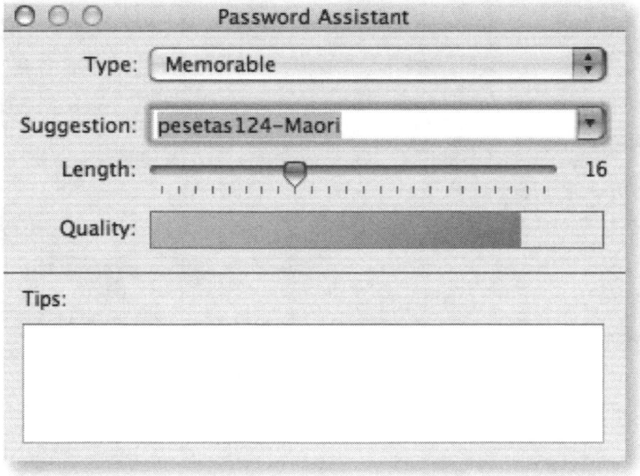

To use Password Assistant, follow these steps:

1. Choose a type from the Type pop-up menu. Most of the choices (Memorable, Letters & Numbers, Numbers Only, Random) are relatively self-explanatory. The choice FIPS-181 Compliant creates passwords that comply with the U.S. Department of Commerce standard. The options Memorable and Random may also include punctuation.

2. Move the slider to the desired password length.

3. If you don't like the automatically generated choice in the Suggestion field, click the arrow at the right of the field to see other options, or choose More Suggestions to generate even more. For each password, the Quality bar fills up farther to the right as the password becomes harder to guess (either by a person or a computer).

6 Things You Might Never Need to Do

Careful readers may have noticed that I omitted two common tasks from my recommendations of periodic maintenance procedures: repairing permissions and defragmenting your hard disk. Read this chapter to discover why you might never need to do these things—or whether you're one of the few people who should.

Repair Permissions

If you visit Mac discussion forums, blogs, and news sites, you've probably seen repeated recommendations to use Disk Utility's Repair Permissions feature. Some people recommend repairing permissions on a daily basis, or before and after every software installation, or as a first troubleshooting step when any sort of problem arises. Anecdotes abound about the seemingly magical curative (or prophylactic) properties of this feature, so it has achieved a sort of mythical status—in much the same way rebuilding the desktop file was a standard cure-all under Mac OS 9.

At the risk of being labeled a heretic, I'd like to suggest that in most cases repairing permissions is nothing more than a placebo. True, the procedure can solve certain problems and rarely does any harm, but as a routine maintenance task, I consider it a waste of time. To explain why, I should provide a bit of background.

In Mac OS X, each file contains information specifying which users (or parts of the system) can read it, modify it, or execute it. This information is collectively known as permissions. If a file has incorrect permissions, it can cause applications to misbehave in various ways, such as crashing or failing to launch.

Ordinarily, installers set the correct permissions for the files they install, and the permissions stay that way permanently. However, a poorly written installer can mess up permissions—even for files it did not install—and if you use Unix commands such as chown and chmod, you can accidentally set files' permissions incorrectly. These sorts of problems occur infrequently, but they do occur.

The Repair Permissions feature looks for software installed using Apple's installer, which leaves behind files called *receipts* that list the locations and initial permissions of all the files in a given package. Repair Permissions compares the current permissions to those listed in the receipts and, if it finds any differences, changes the files back. The command ignores software installed in other ways (using a different installer or drag-and-drop installation, for instance) and knows nothing about legitimate permission changes you may have made deliberately.

Although I said earlier that some kinds of disk problems can occur without any provocation (see the sidebar *Why Do Disk Errors Occur?,* page 50), permissions don't go out of whack all by themselves; you (or software you install) must do something to change them. And not all changes are bad; in many cases, a file's permissions can be different from what they were originally without causing any problems. So repairing permissions makes little sense as a regular activity.

Note: I should mention that Apple suggests repairing disk permissions after installing new software. I suspect that their reason for doing so is to head off tech support calls about problems resulting from the use of a few poorly written third-party installers.

I do, however, recommend repairing permissions as a *troubleshooting* step if (especially right after installing new software) you find that an application no longer launches, or produces inexplicable error messages. To repair permissions, follow these steps:

1. Open Disk Utility (in /Applications/Utilities).

2. Select a volume in the list on the left.

3. In the First Aid view, click Repair Disk Permissions.

Disk Utility resets the permissions of files installed using Apple's installer.

Tip: For much more detail about working with permissions, I recommend reading Brian Tanaka's *Take Control of Permissions in Mac OS X* (www.takecontrolbooks.com/permissions-macosx.html).

Defragment Your Hard Disk

As you use your computer, your files gradually become fragmented into smaller segments scattered across your disk. Some people consider this a serious problem and go to great lengths (and expense) to correct it. Before worrying about fragmentation, you should understand how and why it happens—and what the real-world consequences are.

Pretend, for the sake of illustration, that your hard disk consists of exactly ten blocks, and that initially, your disk contains five small files (A, B, C, D, and E), each of which takes up exactly one block. Your disk looks tidy and clean, something like this: ABCDE_____.

If you delete files B and D and add a couple of new files, F and G, your disk looks like this: A_C_EFG___. If you then add a file H that's twice as big as the others, the drive puts it at the end, like so: A_C_EFGHH_. Now let's say file G grows to two blocks in size. There being too little space between F and H, G must split into two segments: A_C_EFGHHG. Finally, if you add file I and delete file F, your disk looks like this: AIC_E_GHHG.

Are you with me so far? Now imagine this happening with hundreds of thousands of files of many different sizes. Some tiny files might occupy just one block, while some huge ones may occupy millions of blocks. The more you read and write files, the more jumbled the data becomes: individual files split into numerous noncontiguous chunks, and lots of small, empty spots where other files once lived. That's fragmentation: the normal state of your hard disk!

Ordinarily, you never notice fragmentation, because Mac OS X keeps track of which parts of which files are where, and automatically reassembles or disassembles them as needed. With modern hard drives, this process is so fast that it's normally imperceptible. Furthermore, starting with Panther, Mac OS X included automatic background defragmentation of smaller (<20 MB) files, so that although files may not be contiguous with each other, at least most of them are in one piece.

The problem occurs when you have programs that must read or write massive amounts of information in real time, such as audio or video recording and editing applications. When these large files become fragmented, the drive's read-write head must physically zip back and forth over the disk to get all the segments, and sometimes the rate at which it does the zipping is too slow to keep up with the amount of data coming in (or going out). The results can include gaps in the data, stuttering, or slow application performance.

For ordinary users, defragmentation is a waste of time unless the fragmentation is extraordinarily severe (as evidenced by long delays in opening and saving files). But if you use high-end audio or video applications regularly, occasional (say, monthly) defragmentation is worthwhile. Several utilities pick up where Mac OS X leaves off, performing thorough defragmentation and making sure all the empty space on the disk is contiguous, in order to squeeze every last bit of performance out of your drive. The process is quite slow, however—and if you're defragmenting large disks, your computer could be effectively out of commission for many hours. I recommend letting the process run overnight (or better yet, over a weekend). Defragmentation is also somewhat risky, since it involves deleting and rewriting almost every file on your drive. A good backup is always essential before undertaking defragmentation.

Note: Related to defragmentation is *optimization,* which means moving the most frequently used files to the portions of the disk that can be accessed most quickly. Most utilities that defragment also optimize.

Utilities that perform defragmentation include:

- **Disk Defrag,** part of SpeedTools Utilities (www.speedtools.com; $100)

- **Drive Genius,** shown in **Figure 9** (www.prosofteng.com; $100)

- **iDefrag** (www.coriolis-systems.com; $30)

- **TechTool Pro** (www.micromat.com; $98)

Figure 9

*Defragmenting hard disks
is one of Drive Genius's
many capabilities.*

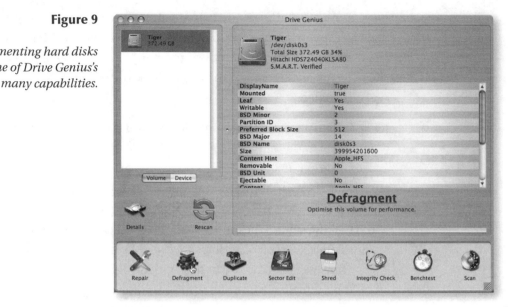

Tip: Another way to defragment your disk is to make a complete, bootable copy (a clone) onto another hard disk, erase the original disk, and then reverse the process, cloning the backup disk onto the original. When the computer writes data to an empty drive, it automatically makes all the files contiguous.

Note that you cannot make a bootable clone simply by dragging files onto another drive. You must use a utility designed to do that job, such as SuperDuper! (www.shirt-pocket.com; $28), Carbon Copy Cloner (www.bombich.com/software/ccc.html; free, donations accepted), or most full-featured backup programs.

---

7 When Apple Releases a New Version of Mac OS X

Every 18 months or so, Apple rolls out a new, major update to Mac OS X. In anticipation a major update, I'd like to share some advice you should follow whenever Apple releases a major new version of Mac OS X.

Note: Even more important than the major upgrades is keeping current with minor updates to Mac OS X, because these are likely to fix serious bugs and security holes. For more information, read *Install the Latest Version of Mac OS X* (page 11) and *Use Software Update to Install Apple Software Updates* (page 42).

Buy It!

For the past several years, Apple has consistently charged $129 for major Mac OS X upgrades. As much as we might all wish they were less expensive, I recommend adding that amount to your budget right now; ultimately, you'll get much more than your money's worth. Major upgrades invariably contain features that enable you to get more done in less time and with less effort. If time is money, upgrades pay for themselves. So plan to make that investment, and it won't seem like such a big deal when the time comes.

Buy *Take Control of Upgrading to* _____

Barring unforeseen problems, I expect that a new version of my electronic book *Take Control of Upgrading to …* will go on sale at exactly the same moment that a major operating system release does. I write these ebooks based on weeks of extensive testing and dozens of installations of the new operating system on numerous test machines. (I've written *Take Control of Upgrading to Panther* and *Take Control of Upgrading to Tiger* so far, and I plan to continue the string with *Take Control of Upgrading to Leopard* and all the rest of Apple's big cats in the future.)

But you're already spending $129 on the operating system itself, so why should you pay even more for an ebook about how to install it? Isn't it just a matter of popping in a DVD and clicking a button. If only it were so. Every upgrade of Mac OS X brings with it not just new features and bug fixes but brand-new hardware and software incompatibilities, installer oddities, and confusing custom installation options. The *Take Control of Upgrading to…* ebooks provide expert guidance through every step of the process, helping you understand every option, keep your data safe, and make sure everything works properly afterward.

Make a Fresh Bootable Backup

Before performing any major system upgrade, be sure to make a new, fresh duplicate of your startup drive (even if you regularly make duplicates once a week). In fact, resources permitting, make two. System upgrades can cause many things to go wrong, and you'll appreciate the security of knowing you can restore your system to its previous state if a problem occurs.

Upgrade

You may be surprised how often someone purchases a Mac OS X upgrade, reads about the installation process, and then leaves the DVD in a drawer for months. Some people habitually wait until the first or second minor update after a major Mac OS X release before taking the plunge, whether to give Apple time to work out all the bugs, to give developers time to up-date their applications for compatibility, or to see how other people like it before committing themselves. And others feel nervous about upgrading until it's nearly time for the *next* major version to be released! Don't let this happen to you.

I'm an early adopter, and although I've experienced my share of minor hurdles, I've never regretted a decision to upgrade immediately. You may, however, wish to delay an upgrade if you're in the middle of a project and can't afford any downtime, if you rely heavily on an application that has not yet been updated to work under the new system, or if you expect to buy a new Mac in the near future (which will, of course, include the latest version of Mac OS X).

8 Monitor Your Mac's Health

No matter how diligently you perform the maintenance tasks I recommend in this book, you won't truly know how well (or how poorly) your Mac is running unless you make the effort to find out. The fact that no smoke is billowing from your SuperDrive is a good sign, of course, but it's hardly definitive proof that all is well. In this chapter, I show you how to find out what's going on under the hood.

Use Monitoring Utilities

Numerous utilities (most of them free) can provide up-to-the-minute vital statistics about your Mac. In most cases, these programs run in the background all the time, but if you prefer, you can run them manually when you get curious about your Mac's current state. I provide a list of several such utilities just ahead. But first, you should understand what information you might want to monitor and why.

RAM Usage

Mac OS X manages your computer's RAM efficiently for the most part. Applications can dynamically adjust the amount of memory they use, and even if all your RAM is actively in use, a virtual memory system lets Mac OS X use a portion of your hard disk to extend your RAM, automatically swapping (or "paging") data between the disk and the physical RAM as needed.

Even so, if you have enough applications open at once, and if they require enough memory to perform their respective tasks, you can get to a point where the data swapping occurs constantly. This slows everything on your Mac way down, and it also uses up disk space.

You should also be aware of a type of bug known as a *memory leak*. Applications usually ask the system for a certain amount of memory for any given task and then give it back when they're done with it. But sometimes, due to a programming error, an application keeps taking memory and not returning any, so that by doing nothing more than staying open, it constantly chews up more and more RAM. You can recover the used memory simply by quitting the application—but you might never know you have this problem in the first place without monitoring your RAM usage.

For all these reasons, I recommend keeping an eye on how much RAM is currently in use. If the free RAM drops near zero, consider closing windows, quitting applications, or even restarting your machine to reduce your Mac's dependence on virtual memory. Better yet, add more RAM (if possible).

Note: In Mac OS X, RAM is not simply "used" or "free" but can be used in any of three different ways: *wired* (in use and crucial to keep your Mac running); *active* (in use now, but may be paged out to disk later); or *inactive* (not currently in use, and possibly paged out to disk, but also stored in RAM for fast access when needed). Most RAM-monitoring utilities break down RAM into these three categories plus "free," and generally include documentation that explains RAM usage in greater detail.

Disk Usage

With hard disk capacity constantly on the rise, you're now less likely to run out of space than you were a few years ago. Nevertheless, the consequences of running out of space can be severe. For one thing, as your hard disk approaches its maximum capacity, your Mac may run more slowly as files become increasingly fragmented. Worse, you could lose data, because your Mac has no space to save a file. And even more seriously, your computer may hang, crash, or fail to start up if it runs out of physical RAM *and* runs out of disk space to use for virtual memory.

In general, I recommend leaving at least 10 to 15 percent of your hard disk space empty to provide breathing room for file storage, virtual memory, disk image creation, and other tasks. When your disk gets close to that level, delete any unneeded files (see the sidebar below for advice about what files to delete), and archive seldom-used files to CD, DVD, or an external hard drive.

Deciding Which Files to Delete

If you find yourself running desperately low on disk space, it may be time to buy a larger hard drive. In the meantime, you can delete files you no longer need. Begin by repeating the procedure in *Clean Out Accumulated Cruft* (page 16). If that still leaves you with too little free disk space and you're stuck for ideas, try removing these items:

Cache files: Mac OS X automatically re-creates these files if needed, so feel free to trash the contents of /Library/Caches and ~/Library/Caches.

Downloads: Do you tend to hang onto installers or other downloaded files that you could simply download again if you

needed to use them? If so, out they go.

Classic resources: If (and only if) you never use Mac OS X's Classic environment, you can get rid of the Mac OS 9 System Folder (but *not* the folder named System, which belongs to Mac OS X!) and any Classic applications (usually they are stored in a folder called "Applications (Mac OS 9)").

Developer tools: If you installed Apple's Xcode Tools but aren't developing any software, you can remove the Developer folder located at the top level of your hard disk. The proper way to do this is to double-click the file

/Developer/Tools/uninstall-devtools.pl.

Re-rippable music: As a last resort, look in ~/Music/iTunes/iTunes Music for music you still have on CD (and which, therefore, you can reimport). While you're at it, toss out old podcasts you no longer need or can download again for free, as well as any tunes you know you'll never listen to again. Be careful not to trash music you purchased from the iTunes Music Store!

When you're finished deleting files, don't forget to empty the Trash (Finder > Empty Trash) to free up the space formerly occupied by those files.

Although you can tell how much free space is on a disk by selecting it in the Finder and choosing File > Get Info, you may not notice if it gets dangerously full while you're busy working. (Mac OS X does display a warning message when space gets critically low, but it appears much too late for my taste.) Several utilities display a live status indicator (in your menu bar, a Dock icon, or a floating window) showing your disks' current free space.

CPU Load

Your Mac contains one or more CPUs—chips that do the bulk of the computer's information processing. Depending on what software is running and what that software is doing, the CPU load goes up and down. Because all your applications share the available CPU power, it's generally true that the higher the overall load, the slower your software will run. In addition, greater CPU load means a higher internal temperature, forcing your computer's fans to work harder.

Having your CPU(s) run at 100 percent capacity from time to time is normal. However, if the load is always at or near maximum—or if it's high even when your computer is relatively inactive—you may have a problem. For example, a background application could have a bug that causes it to use too much processor capacity, slowing down your foreground tasks. Or you may be running more applications than your hardware can handle gracefully. In any case, keeping an eye on CPU usage can help you spot potential problems before they get out of hand. Some CPU monitoring tools display a breakdown of usage by application, so that if one program is hogging too much of the CPU capacity, you can force it to quit.

Temperatures

Extreme heat can damage delicate components inside your Mac. This is why all Macs have carefully designed cooling systems, which usually rely on two or more fans to vent heat away from the processor, hard drive, and other vital components. These fans, in turn, rely on one or more internal temperature sensors that tell them when to turn on or off or to increase or decrease speed.

If a fan malfunctions, if dust blocks the flow of air through your computer, or if a defect in your computer causes it to overheat for some reason, bad things can happen. Your Mac may hang, shut down unexpectedly, or display other improper behavior. Depending on the nature and severity of the problem, you might be looking at an intermittent inconvenience or an expensive trip to the repair shop. In any case, it behooves you to be alert to excessive temperatures.

Several utilities monitor each of your computer's internal temperature sensors, so that you can easily see when heat exceeds safe limits and take action before damage occurs.

Note: The types, positions, and design of temperature sensors vary from one Mac model to the next. Not all Macs' sensors work with monitoring utilities or provide live updates of their readings.

Other Statistics

Some utilities monitor other statistics that may be interesting (though not necessarily relevant to your Mac's health). These include:

♦ Network traffic

♦ Disk access activity

♦ Battery level (for portables)

♦ System uptime (time since the computer was last turned on or re-started)

Monitoring Utilities

Although this is by no means an exhaustive list, the following utilities all provide one or more monitoring services:

♦ **Activity Monitor:** This utility, included as part of Mac OS X (in `/Applications/Utilities`) displays CPU load, RAM usage, disk activity and usage, and network traffic (see **Figure 10**).

Figure 10

Activity Monitor, included with Mac OS X, displays CPU and RAM usage, among numerous other statistics.

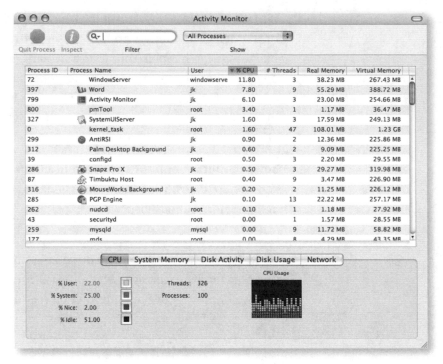

Activity Monitor also displays memory and CPU usage statistics for each running application, and enables you to quit individual applications. Although it includes an optional floating CPU window, Activity Monitor is not the best choice for background operation.

♦ **Amnesia:** This tiny application displays current CPU load and free memory (only) in its Dock icon (`http://dockapp-osx.sourceforge.net/dockapps.html`, free).

♦ **App Monitor:** If you want to keep an eye on the CPU usage of one application at a time, try App Monitor (`http://blazingmousesoft.free.fr/`, free), which displays a customizable usage graph in either a window or a Dock icon.

♦ **Hardware Monitor:** This utility can display a wide variety of statistics in your menu bar, a Dock icon, or several other formats. Information includes heat sensor readings, power supply voltage and current, fan speeds (in RPM), battery level, and other data, depending on your Mac model (`www.bresink.com/osx/HardwareMonitor.html`; $7).

+ **Mac HelpMate:** In addition to performing many maintenance tasks, this utility displays free RAM, internal temperature readings, disk usage, S.M.A.R.T. status, and system uptime (`www.macworkshops.com/machelpmate/`; free, donations accepted).

+ **MemoryStick:** This simple utility from Matt Neuburg displays a floating bar graph showing your current RAM usage (`www.tidbits.com/matt/`; free).

+ **Memory Usage Getter:** Somewhat along the lines of Activity Monitor, this utility displays overall RAM usage, plus per-application RAM and CPU usage, and enables you to quit individual applications (`http://homepage.mac.com/simx/`; $10).

+ **MenuMeters:** My favorite utility of the group, MenuMeters (`www.ragingmenace.com`; free), shown in **Figure 11**, adds tiny, customizable indicators to your menu bar to display any or all of the following: CPU load, RAM usage, disk access activity (with usage on a drop-down menu), and network traffic.

Figure 11

MenuMeters can display RAM and CPU usage, as well as numerous other bits of information, in highly configurable menus.

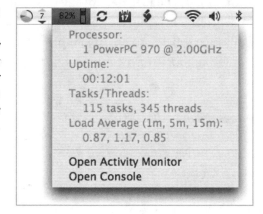

+ **miniStat:** For Dashboard fans, this collection of six Dashboard widgets (`http://shockwidgets.com/`; free) displays CPU load, free RAM, free disk space, CPU temperature, battery level, and system uptime.

+ **iStat pro:** Another Dashboard widget, iStat pro (`www.islayer.net`; free) displays a single panel with the following information: CPU load, RAM usage, network traffic (and bandwidth), disk usage, battery level, and system uptime.

♦ **Temperature Monitor:** This utility displays readings from your Mac's internal heat sensors, and even produces a graph of the temperatures over time (www.bresink.com/osx/TemperatureMonitor.html; free).

♦ **ThermographX:** This utility (www.kezer.net/thermographx.html; $7) displays the readings of all internal heat sensors in your Mac and even keeps a graph of the temperature over time. But it's not compatible with every Mac model.

♦ **X Resource Graph:** XRG (www.gauchosoft.com; free) provides highly customizable graphs of CPU usage, RAM usage, disk access activity, network traffic, internal heat sensors (up to three), and battery level, plus weather (in a city of your choice) and stock market data.

Check Your Drives' S.M.A.R.T. Status

Most modern hard drives have built-in sensors and monitoring circuitry that form a system called S.M.A.R.T. (Self-Monitoring Analysis and Reporting Technology). The idea of S.M.A.R.T. is to detect the warning signs of potential problems *before* they occur. Although S.M.A.R.T. cannot detect every possible drive problem, it can provide one very valuable warning: "Your drive is about to have problems, so back it up and repair (or replace) it now!"

What does it work with? As of mid 2006, Disk Utility's S.M.A.R.T. indicator works with internal ATA and Serial ATA drives, but not with external (USB or FireWire) drives. Some external drives, however, have their own built-in S.M.A.R.T. indicators.

To check your drives' S.M.A.R.T. status, launch Disk Utility (find it in /Applications/Utilities) and select a drive in the list on the left. (Be sure to select the drive itself, not one of the indented volumes beneath it.) If the selected drive supports S.M.A.R.T., you should see this at the bottom of the window: "S.M.A.R.T. Status: Verified" (**Figure 12**). If you see "About to Fail" in red letters, back up the drive immediately. You can then use Disk Utility (or a third-party repair utility) to attempt to repair the drive, but more often than not, "About to Fail" indicates an imminent hardware failure that you cannot fix with software. Even if Disk Utility does appear to solve the problem, don't trust the drive with important data; replace it as soon as possible.

Figure 12

Disk Utility shows a drive's S.M.A.R.T. status.

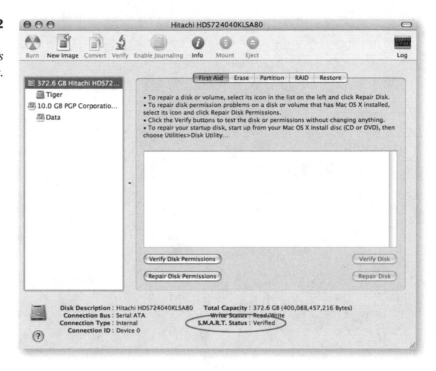

Tip: To monitor your drives' S.M.A.R.T. status in the background (without having to remember to open Disk Utility), try SMARTReporter, which displays a status icon in your menu bar (`http://homepage.mac.com/julianmayer/`, free).

9 Decide on a Backup Strategy

I know a number of people who have made decisions about backing up their computers based on what hardware or software they already own. Others buy a product that's received good reviews and then figure out how to use it for effective backups. I believe these approaches are backward. If your data and your time are truly important, it makes sense to think about your needs first, then develop a strategy based on those needs, and finally choose hardware and software that fits your strategy.

When earlier versions of this manuscript were published, several readers commented that the strategy I suggest here, while perfectly reasonable, may be inappropriate for "low-end" users because it presumes a significant expenditure of money and effort. Less-advanced users, the argument went, just want a backup system that's inexpensive, easy-to-use, and effective. Don't we all! Unfortunately, there is no such thing. You know the old saying: "Cheap; good; fast—pick any two." The same goes for backups. I can tell you how to do them effectively or how to do them quickly and cheaply, but the less time and money you're willing to spend, the less safe your data will be.

With that in mind, I want to begin this strategy section with a quick, high-level overview of several approaches you might choose to take, depending on your tolerance for cost, effort, and risk (see **Table 1**, "Sample Backup Approaches"). Later on, I describe in detail each of the hardware, software, and strategic components of these options.

While the approaches I outline are just a few examples of the many paths one could take to performing backups, I personally feel the importance of protecting your data trumps all other concerns. Therefore, in **Table 1**, I outlined the Data Safety approach in bold, because I believe it is the best approach for the majority of readers of this book. If your data is not worth some time and money to you, then you probably don't need backups. But if data safety truly matters—can you afford to lose your email, one-of-a-kind digital photos, or important documents?—keep in mind that you get out of a backup system what you put into it.

Table 1: Sample Backup Approaches		
Major Objective	**Suggested Approach**	**Risks and Trade-Offs**
Saving Money	◆ Hardware: Your Mac's built-in SuperDrive. ◆ Software: Tri-Backup ($49). ◆ Strategy: Schedule weekly duplicates and daily archives, and store them on DVD-RW or DVD+RW.	◆ You will not have a bootable duplicate, making it more difficult to recover after a hard drive failure. ◆ You must be present when backups occur to swap media. ◆ Restoring files from an archive will be time-consuming.
Ease of Use	◆ Hardware: A single Maxtor OneTouch FireWire drive. ◆ Software: Retrospect Express. ◆ Strategy: Just press the button for instant (duplicate) backups whenever you wish.	◆ No archives to protect you against file changes and deletions, unless you set up such a script manually. ◆ Without redundant, off-site media, you risk data loss due to theft, fire, or other catastrophes. ◆ You must remember to press the button.
	AND/OR	
	◆ Use an *Internet* backup service such as Prolifix, which provides its own software and requires no hardware.	◆ No bootable duplicates. ◆ Extremely expensive if you archive all your files; significant risk of data loss if you do not. ◆ Your data is unavailable if you lose Internet connectivity.
Data Safety	◆ Hardware: Three external FireWire drives. ◆ Software: Retrospect Desktop. ◆ Strategy: Scheduled weekly duplicates and daily archives, alternating among drives; one drive always stored off-site. ◆ Optional: Archive mission-critical and active files frequently to your iDisk or an Internet backup service.	◆ Significant hardware and software costs. ◆ Learning curve to set up and use Retrospect software. ◆ Inconvenience of moving drives around each week.

Tip: There's an even more secure level beyond the "Data Safety" option in **Table 1**, but implementing it takes a bit of doing. Make these modifications to the plan:

♦ Use hardware-encrypted hard drives (see *Choosing a Hard Drive*, page 121).

♦ Using SoftRAID, partition each of the external drives into a volume for archives and a volume for duplicates (see *Can a RAID Substitute for Duplicates?*, page 92).

♦ Rotate the drives more frequently (say, once every two or three days) and keep one or more of them offsite at all times.

Do You Need Duplicates?

Let's begin by assuming you have original (CD-ROM or DVD-ROM) copies of your operating system and all installed software. Now consider this question:

If your hard drive suffered a complete failure, how much time could you afford to spend restoring it to working order?

If you use your computer to run a business, do your homework, or trade stocks, for example, your answer may be "a few minutes at the most." If no critical projects depend on a functional computer, you may be able to afford several days to restore it after a failure. Most of us are somewhere in between.

In the best case, it will take you several hours—and possibly a day or more—to reinstall a typical set of software onto a new or reformatted disk. However, if you do not have original copies of all your software, if you have a large number of third-party applications, or if you've customized your computer extensively, returning your computer to operation could take much longer.

The more you need to avoid that potential loss of time, the more you need to maintain duplicates (for more info, see *The Duplicate*, page 92).

Do You Need Archives?

Regardless of your need for duplicates, consider your answer to this much different question:

If your computer were stolen, how difficult would it be for you to live without the data on it?

Do you have years of bank records, email, poetry, academic papers, photos, movies, and so on stored on your computer? If so, chances are your answer is "extremely difficult." On the other hand, if you use your computer only for casual Web surfing, playing games, and listening to music, living without the data on your computer may be little more than a minor inconvenience.

Although a duplicate includes a copy of your data, an archive includes many different versions of your data, making it much more likely that you'll be able to retrieve the information you need in the event of a problem.

The greater the amount of personal data on your computer—and its importance to you—the greater your need to maintain archives (for more info, see *The Archive,* page 94).

Though there may be some exceptions, the ideal backup strategy for most people consists of both duplicates and archives. I discuss each of these in the pages that follow.

Do You Have Special Backup Needs?

Although duplicates and archives cover most situations the typical user will encounter, some people have special backup needs that don't quite fit the mold. I'm thinking, in particular, of users with large numbers of digital photos and those who work extensively with the large files required for digital video or pro audio applications.

Digital Photos

Many people, when asked what one item they would try to save if their house were burning down, would answer "my photo album"—because furniture can be replaced, but memories cannot. The same thing is true of the memories stored on your hard disk in the form of pictures you've taken with your digital camera.

Most of us have at least a few digital photos on our computers. But some people take pictures constantly, and feel justifiably concerned about entrusting this irreplaceable data to their computers. Also, digital camera resolution is constantly on the rise—meaning the next new camera you buy is going to require more space for the same number of images as your previous one. Your new mobile phone probably has a camera, too. As the number and size of your images increases, you may find that duplicates and archives alone don't entirely meet your backup needs.

For one thing, it can be extraordinarily difficult to find just the right photo from among thousands of similarly named files when it comes time to restore your data from a backup. Although Spotlight can use keywords and other metadata to help you find photos when they're on your hard disk, it won't help you when they're on a stack of DVDs. (For solutions to this problem, see *Cataloging software,* page 107.)

Photos are also among the files you're most likely to share with other people. If you've ever created an online photo album using iPhoto, iWeb, or .Mac HomePage, you know how easy (and addictive) photo sharing can be. Although the files you've shared on the Web do, in a sense, constitute a backup of the ones on your computer, you probably haven't shared *all* your files online—and you most likely uploaded low-resolution copies of the images anyway. Wouldn't it be great if you could back up all your photos online, and still have the ability to share just the ones you want? (You can! I explain how in *Photo-sharing services*, page 108.)

Finally, let's not forget that photos are especially valuable. Although you wouldn't enjoy spending months rewriting The Great American Novel, it's at least possible. Recreating photos of a new baby or an important life event, on the other hand, simply can't be done.

Luckily, numerous tools, services, and strategies exist for the express purpose of making photo backups as painless and secure as possible. To learn more about them, read *Photo Backup Strategy* (page 107).

Video and Audio

Video files consume an enormous amount of disk space, and when you're working on editing a large video project or producing DVDs, the file sizes can become truly staggering. Add HD video content to the mix, and the file sizes balloon even further. Because of the sheer quantity of data you may generate, conventional duplicates and archives may not make the most sense. You're also likely to create numerous intermediate files between the raw footage and the final product, and deciding whether or how to back up that data can be challenging.

All this is equally true for those working with audio production, especially when your Mac functions as a multitrack recorder; it also holds for photographers working with gigantic, ultra-high-resolution images and several other categories of user.

So ask yourself this question:

Do you frequently generate more than a few gigabytes of new or modified files in a single day?

If you're working with large video, audio, or still image files, the answer is likely yes. All that data can strain conventional backup methods, not to mention your pocketbook. Learn more about how to get the job done without breaking the bank in *Video and Audio Backup Strategy* (page 110).

The Duplicate

Whether you call it a clone, a bootable backup, a mirror, or a carbon copy, a *duplicate* is a complete, exact copy of your entire hard disk that (if it's stored on, or restored onto, a hard disk) you can use to start up your computer if necessary. Duplicates are wonderful because they enable you to get back up and running extremely quickly—in some cases, with only minutes of down time.

Consider this typical scenario: you've duplicated your Mac's internal hard disk onto a FireWire drive. One day your computer won't start at all; the screen displays a blinking question mark indicating that it can't find a valid system. You suspect a catastrophic hard disk crash. No problem: you

Can a RAID Substitute for Duplicates?

RAID stands for Redundant Array of Independent (or Inexpensive) Disks; it's a way of combining multiple physical hard drives into a single logical volume using either software or a special hardware controller. One way to configure a RAID, known as *mirroring,* is to have the same data written simultaneously to two or more drives. If any one drive fails, another can take over instantly and seamlessly with no loss of data and no down time; you can then replace the faulty drive at your leisure.

I have nothing against RAIDs, and if you need to keep a mission-critical computer running without any hiccups at all, a mirrored RAID might be just what you need. However, I strongly believe that a RAID, by itself, is no substitute for multiple duplicates as described in this book. The best

feature of a mirrored RAID is also its Achilles' heel: because changes are reflected on all drives simultaneously, an accidentally deleted file will be immediately deleted on your "backup" drives too! (Stand-alone duplicates—especially if you maintain two or three of them—reduce this risk greatly.) RAIDs address the problem of spontaneous drive failures, but they provide no insurance against human error, theft, natural disaster, or any of the other catastrophes that make backups so important.

That said, you *can* have your cake and eat it too (for a price). If you use SoftRAID (www.softraid.com; $129), you can create a RAID in which your internal hard disk is mirrored onto *two or more* external drives at once. You can then periodically rotate one of the drives off-site,

where it will function as a stand-alone duplicate of your hard disk at an earlier state. When you plug it back into your computer, it will automatically synchronize itself with the remaining drives in the RAID. The beauty of this approach is that you never have to set up, schedule, or run backup software to make duplicates—it just happens automatically.

This scheme can even be expanded to include archives. Using SoftRAID, it is possible (though awkward) to partition an external drive in such a way that one partition can be used along with your internal drive to form a mirrored RAID while another, non-RAID partition on the external can hold archives. Set up two external drives this way and you're in business—as close to a painless backup system as I can imagine.

quickly hook up your backup drive and boot from that. Your computer will behave exactly as if it were running from the internal disk, with the exception that files added or changed since you performed the backup will be missing or out of date. You can then repair the internal disk—or if it's completely dead, simply replace it.

You might think it would take a while to make a copy of your entire hard disk, and you'd be right. But most software capable of making a bootable duplicate can also duplicate *incrementally*—meaning that after the first time, updating your duplicate to reflect the current state of your hard disk requires only copying files that are new or different. Because duplicates are so powerful and useful, I recommend that you make them part of your backup strategy.

However, due to the proliferation and simplicity of synchronization utilities, many people use duplicates as their *only* backup (see the sidebar *Synchronization Utilities,* page 94). This is a bad idea. Here's why:

♦ Duplicates provide no insurance against damaged or accidentally deleted files. If your hard disk is missing files, or contains damaged files, when you perform the duplication, those problems will appear in the duplicate as well.

♦ Duplicates quickly go out of date. Even while your backup is in progress, files may change. So if your only backup is a duplicate, you may increase your risk that backed-up files will not be current.

For these reasons, although I urge you to duplicate your hard disk regularly, you should supplement the duplicates with archives (as I describe in *The Archive,* page 94).

Note: An extra hard drive is certainly the *best* way to make a duplicate, but you can also duplicate a volume onto a disk image, which can be stored on removable media such as CD-R or DVD-R—and then restored onto a hard drive when needed. By the way, it is possible, though not easy, to make a bootable Mac OS X CD or DVD. Because this process goes far beyond normal backups, I do not cover it here.

The Archive

Sometimes referred to simply as a *backup*, an *archive* contains copies of your files as they appeared at multiple points in time. If you want to see the version of a file that existed on your computer 2 weeks ago, an archive can deliver that—along with today's version and the version that existed a month ago.

An archive starts with a complete copy of all the files in one or more folders. The next time the backup runs, your backup software could make another complete copy, but because most of the files probably have not changed in the meantime, that would use up a great deal of space—not to mention taking a long time. So backup programs typically perform an *incremental archive*. This means that on subsequent runs, the software scans the files in the folders you've designated and copies only those files that are new (or newly modified) since the last backup. To be truly useful, archives should also be *additive*, meaning the backup program adds the new or changed

Synchronization Utilities

Lots of utilities—including several that bill themselves as backup tools—perform synchronization. As the name implies, *synchronization* means maintaining identical copies of a file, folder, or even an entire disk in two or more locations. Some synchronization utilities can run on a schedule, automatically "backing up" files from a location you specify to another volume. And some can create a bootable duplicate by synchronizing an entire disk to another disk.

There's nothing wrong with synchronization—in fact, it can be incredibly useful in certain circumstances, such as keeping your laptop's hard disk updated with documents you use frequently on your desktop Mac. As a quick and easy way of making an extra copy of certain files, it can serve as a type of primitive backup.

If you want to use a synchronization utility to make duplicates as part of your backup strategy, that is perfectly valid too. However, please do not mistake synchronization for a true backup—no matter what the utility's advertising says.

What's true of duplicates is equally true of individually synchronized files and folders: you get only the most recently modified version. You lack the ability to recover an older version of the file, which is a crucial part of a solid backup program. Also, if you don't notice that a file is damaged before synchronizing it to another volume, you may end up with two useless copies. If you synchronize deletions, you lose your insurance against accidentally trashing files. And it's all too easy to accidentally copy data in the wrong direction!

All that to say: a single copy of a single version of your data does not a backup make. By all means, synchronize if you wish, but not as a substitute for proper archives and complete, bootable duplicates.

files to the archive without overwriting the files already there. That way, you can retrieve many different versions of a given file, and if you delete it on your hard disk, you can still find it in your archive. Thus, what I refer to as an archive is technically an *additive incremental archive*.

Note: Some backup programs use the term *archive* to describe files that have been copied to removable media of some kind for long-term storage and then deleted from the source volume.

Archives sometimes make use of a *snapshot*—a list of all the files in the designated folders at the time a backup runs. Even though a certain file may not be copied (because it hasn't changed since the last backup), it will appear in the snapshot list. You can easily see what the entire contents of a folder looked like at various arbitrary points in the past, and restore it to any previous state in a single operation.

After the initial full backup, archives usually take comparatively little time to run, making it easy to back up your data once (or even several times) each day. This ensures that your most recent backup is never more than a day old. Because they also offer tremendous insurance against accidental deletion (or change) and file damage, archives are an essential part of a good backup strategy. But archives alone are not an adequate solution. I say this for two main reasons:

♦ Because of the way archives are stored, they do not represent a complete, intact version of your entire hard disk. Ordinarily, an archive is not bootable (at least, not until after you've restored it to a fresh disk). If your main hard drive is completely dead, you won't be able to do any work at all until you've replaced it.

♦ It often makes sense for an archive to include only data files—not your operating system or applications (*Archive Strategy*, page 105, discusses the pros and cons of such an approach). But reinstalling Mac OS X and applications from their original CDs or DVDs is a lengthy and cumbersome process that you could avoid (or speed up dramatically) with a duplicate of your hard disk.

Archives protect you against inadvertent changes over time, but only a duplicate can get you up and running again quickly after a major problem. In other words, the best backup strategy includes both duplicates and archives.

That said, you can set up both duplicates and archives in many different ways, depending on the hardware and software you have, the types and sizes of files you typically work with, and other variables. I make some general suggestions ahead under *Joe's Recommended Strategy* (page 104), and I provide more detailed instructions in Chapter 12.

Scheduling Backups

I can say from personal experience that backups are far more likely to happen regularly if your backup software runs automatically on a schedule. And let me be quite clear: *regular* backups are the only kind that matter. I think it's fair to state this as a corollary to Murphy's Law: "The likelihood of suffering data loss increases in direct proportion to the elapsed time since your last backup." In other words, if you're performing all your backups manually, the one day you forget (or run out of time) will be the day something goes wrong.

Incremental or Differential?

Some backup programs distinguish between incremental and differential archiving schemes. Although not all software uses the terms in exactly the same way, the difference is typically that in an incremental backup, only the files changed or added since the last time the backup ran are added to the archive. With a differential backup, all the files changed or added since the initial full backup are added to the archive. Thus, differential backups take longer to run than incremental backups.

This distinction is important when backing up to tapes or other removable media, because it affects the speed with which a backup can be restored. When restoring from an incremental backup, the software must copy the entire initial backup and then step through each of the incremental backups to retrieve all the updated files. This can require a great deal of media swapping. A differential backup, on the other hand, can be restored more quickly because the software must copy only the original backup and the most recent one.

When backing up to a hard drive, however, this distinction is less significant, because the random-access nature of a hard drive enables it to restore either sort of backup with roughly equal speed.

One consideration in choosing a backup schedule is media management. For example, if you're backing up to a recordable DVD, you must be prepared to insert a blank disc whenever the schedule runs. Swapping media can be an intrusion into your normal routine (especially if that routine involves the frequent use of other discs in the drive you use for backups). On the other hand, if you schedule backups to run when you're not around, you must always think ahead and make sure the drive has the necessary media ready. If, on the other hand, you're backing up to a hard disk or network device that can stay connected all the time, this problem occurs less frequently, if at all.

Depending on the speed of your computer, which software you use, and how you configure it, you may find that your computer slows down significantly while backups are running. This could be an argument for scheduling backups for when you're not using the machine. However, if you do not leave your computer on all the time, you will need to take special care to ensure that it's on and ready when the backups are scheduled to run (see the sidebar *Power Management and Backups*, page 171, for more information).

How often should you back up your computer? And if you're making both duplicates and archives, how often should you update each?

No single answer is right for everyone, but as a starting point, my rule of thumb is that duplicates should be updated *at least* as frequently as major changes to your system (such as installing Mac OS X updates or new versions of applications), and archives should be updated every day you make minor changes (receiving email, modifying text documents, and so on). Thus, if you use your computer heavily every day, and often install new or updated software, you might opt for weekly updates of your duplicates and daily updates of your archives. On the other hand, if you use your computer only occasionally, the schedule could become once a month for duplicates and once or twice a week for archives. Under no circumstances do I suggest backing up less frequently than once a month or more frequently than twice a day—the risk is too high in the former case and the aggravation too great in the latter.

Tip: Always update your duplicate just *before* installing system software updates. That way, if the new version of the software contains any serious problems, you can easily roll back your system to its previous state.

There may be some cases in which you could not afford to lose even a half day's work in the event of a serious problem, making twice-daily archives seem inadequate. If you're working on an important document, there's nothing wrong with copying it to another volume once per hour or as often as you feel it's necessary—or scheduling your backup software or a synchronization utility to do so for you. But updating an entire archive that frequently is likely to slow your work.

For more specifics about configuring your backup software to run on a schedule, read *Automate Your Backups,* page 170.

Keeping Multiple Backups

A sound backup strategy always includes backups of your backups! Picture this: you've diligently backed up your computer's internal hard disk to an external drive. Then one day, lightning strikes and *both* drives are damaged—or your home is robbed and all your equipment stolen. So much for your backup. Backup media can fail for all the same reasons your hard drive can fail. So having just one backup, in my opinion, is never enough. You should alternate between two or more sets of backup media for greater safety. If you've set up your backups to run on a schedule, this might mean using set A (a hard drive or a stack of CDs) every day for a week, then switching to set B (a different drive or stack of CDs) for each day of the following week, then switching back—and so on.

So are *two* sets enough? It depends. Most experts recommend using at least three sets, of which one is always stored off-site. But this advice was first given in the days when the media commonly used for backups was much less reliable than what's available today. And the cost of three sets of media—especially hard drives—can be hard to swallow for the average home or small-business Mac user.

In my opinion, except for mission-critical business use, two sets each of duplicates and archives should be adequate for most users. If you back up to hard drives, this can mean two drives, each of which is partitioned to store both a duplicate and an archive. Of course, if you can afford a third set, your data will be somewhat safer—and your backup routine will be somewhat easier. In any case, you certainly should keep one of those sets in another location all the time.

Backing Up a Small Network

To this point, I've assumed that you're backing up a single Mac. But what if you have several in your home or office? How does this affect your backup strategy?

One approach is to back up each machine separately. This may involve keeping separate stacks of recordable CDs or DVDs next to each machine, or hooking up external FireWire drives to each one (though you could, of course, move a single high-capacity drive from one computer to the next). If your backup needs are relatively small, there's nothing wrong with this approach. But if you have more than a couple of machines—especially if their hard disks contain a lot of data that you can't afford to lose—a wiser strategy would be to back them all up at the same time over your network.

Note: You do have a network, right? If you have multiple machines that aren't currently connected (whether by Ethernet cabling or AirPort wireless networking), you should hook them up. Not only does a network enable better backups, it makes transferring files and accessing the Internet much easier.

Network Backup Approaches

In a network backup, one computer functions as the backup server. This is the machine to which your backup device(s) are physically connected. Files from your other machines are copied over the network onto each backup device. Network backups can proceed by three different methods:

◆ The server shares its backup volume (using AFP, FTP, or SMB; see the Glossary for info on these acronyms), which the client machines mount as a volume in the Finder. Then each client machine uses its own backup application to back up files to the network volume (rather than a locally attached hard drive or optical drive). This is sometimes called a *push* backup, as each client "pushes" its data onto the network volume.

◆ Each client machine shares its hard disk (again, using AFP, FTP, or SMB). The server mounts each of these volumes in the Finder, and then the single copy of the backup application running on the server copies files from each of the network volumes onto its locally attached backup volume. This is sometimes called a *pull* backup, as the server "pulls" data from each of the clients onto its backup volumes.

◆ The server runs backup software that supports *client-server* network backups, and the other machines run client software that communicates with the server directly—without any of the machines having to share or mount volumes.

Note: Some SMB servers limit the size of any single file to 2 GB; others limit it to 4 GB; still others have limits as high as 2 TB. Because some backup software transmits *all* your data over the network as a single file, you may run into situations where you cannot back up more than 2 GB (or 4 GB) of data to an SMB server. If you can't persuade your system administrator to update the server software to a version that supports larger file sizes, you may need to use a different server (or different backup software).

Almost all backup applications support push and pull network backups, but I recommend against them. For one thing, network volumes can become disconnected for any number of reasons, and if a volume is unavailable when it's time for a scheduled backup, that backup will fail. A few applications can try to mount missing volumes for you (even remembering user names and passwords, if necessary), but even this is no guarantee of success. Push and pull backups are also inherently less secure than client-server backups, and are sometimes quite slow. Also, in the case of pull backups, file ownership may change in unacceptable ways, making bootable backups impossible. Sometimes push backups can be bootable, but it's a dicey operation.

True client-server backups require less effort, are more secure, and tend to offer more flexibility. Often, client-server backup software also supports multiple platforms. Of the backup software covered in this book, Retrospect, RsyncX, and BackupSW offer client-server backups. Retrospect and BackupSW both support Mac OS X and Windows; Retrospect also supports Mac OS 9, while BackupSW also supports Linux.

If you need to back up a small Macintosh or Macintosh/Windows network, I recommend Retrospect Desktop, which includes a license to back up the machine on which it's installed, plus two more client computers (additional client licenses are available at $37 each, with volume discounts if purchased in packs of 5, 10, 50, or 100). You'll get the best results with the Backup Server script (see *Set Up a Backup Server Script,* page 200), using hard disks that are large enough for all the data on all the Macs (see *Does Size Matter?,* page 118).

Special Considerations

Besides selecting the right software, several other matters require your attention when planning a network backup system:

♦ **Media:** Although optical media or other removable storage may be acceptable for single-machine backups, for best results, network backups require storage devices that are always available. In other words, hard drives are the best bet for small networks. (See Chapter 10.) Also, if you're making duplicates that you may later wish to boot from, be sure to partition the hard disks in such a way that each startup disk on the network gets its own partition for a duplicate.

♦ **Bandwidth:** You can perform a network backup using an AirPort wireless network, but even with AirPort Extreme, you get only a small percentage of the bandwidth that a wired 100Base-T Ethernet connection will give you—so backups will take much longer, especially if you're duplicating an entire hard disk. In any case, you definitely want the highest-bandwidth network connection you can get. If your computer uses multiple network interfaces, open System Preferences, go to the Network pane, and choose Network Port Configurations from the Show pop-up menu. In the list that appears, drag Built-in Ethernet to the top and click Apply Now to ensure that the wired network is used in preference to AirPort when both are available.

Note: Every network is different, but I have seen cases where Retrospect client-server backups are unreliable when the client machines' IP addresses are dynamically assigned by an AirPort base station. If this happens to you, consider assigning (private) static IP addresses to each client.

♦ **Availability:** For a scheduled network backup to occur, both server and client machines must be turned on and awake. If your machines are currently not left on all the time, check the Energy Saver pane in System Preferences on each computer to ensure that it will not be off or asleep when backups occur. (For more info, read the sidebar *Power Management and Backups,* page 171.)

Tip: Scheduling network backups for times when all machines are available can be a challenge—particularly if you have laptop computers that are not always on the network. Retrospect offers a great feature called Backup Server that constantly polls all the clients on a network. If it sees one that hasn't been backed up in at least 24 hours (or a period of time you specify), it performs the backup right away. That way, you needn't set up an exact schedule for each machine. Backup Server can be restricted to run only during certain hours on certain days, and it can also use any available, designated hard disk as a destination—so you don't need to figure out in advance when to swap media (for more information, read *Set Up a Backup Server Script,* page 200).

Remote Backups

In the discussion so far, I've assumed that the machines you need to back up are connected to the same local network as your backup server. But what if you travel frequently with a laptop? Can you use a broadband connection at a hotel or Internet café to copy the files to your server over the Internet? The short answer is: Maybe.

"Push" backups work only if you can mount your backup server's volumes remotely; "pull" backups work only if your server can mount your laptop's volume remotely. Sometimes this works, but often not—your firewall at home must enable access to the necessary ports, and the ISP providing your remote access must also permit file-sharing access over their network. You also run a certain risk that your files may be intercepted in transit by a hacker, unless you take extra steps to encrypt the network link between your laptop and your server.

Client-server backup software, such as Retrospect, normally polls only the local network for available clients. In some cases—for example, with the more-expensive Retrospect Workgroup or Retrospect Server packages—you can manually enter an IP address for a computer outside your local network. However, if you're traveling and don't know what IP address you'll have at any given time, this method is problematic. One possible solution is to use a dynamic DNS service, such as the one provided by easyDNS (www.easydns.com/dynamicdns.php3), to assign your laptop a domain name whose IP address changes as needed, and then enter that domain name in Retrospect.

This problem is more readily solvable using a VPN (virtual private network) connection to your home network, but the details of setting up such a system go beyond what I can cover in this book. As a lower-tech workaround, consider packing some DVD-R media for temporary backups when you're on the road—and be sure to store the discs separately from your laptop!

Joe's Recommended Strategy

What I recommend for most users is a two-pronged approach: periodically scheduled (say, weekly) duplicates of your entire hard disk, and even more frequent (say, daily) archives of your data files.

The duplicates will provide you with a complete, bootable copy of your hard disk, while the archives will pick up all the files that change regularly. Users with extensive photo or video data may need to go a step or two further—separating that data from their main backups and using special strategies to keep it safe without incurring enormous media and equipment expenses.

Duplication Strategy

You should create duplicates (onto hard drives, ideally) of your primary disk and any other startup volume you normally use. If you have a single, unpartitioned hard disk, then you have only a single volume to worry about. If you have multiple partitions (or multiple internal or external hard drives) that contain bootable systems, I recommend making duplicates of *all of them*. If a hard drive fails, after all, it can take with it all the partitions it contains; and a disaster that wipes out a single drive could wipe out all of your drives.

Note: When you create a duplicate, you copy *everything* from the source drive to the target drive—including, of course, all the files that make up Mac OS X. Therefore, there is no need to install Mac OS X on your external drive before creating a duplicate.

Most duplication software enables you to deselect individual folders you wish to exclude from a duplicate; some use selectors, exclusions, or both (see *Selectors and Exclusions,* page 147). Although you could make an argument that some files are not worth including in a duplicate (such as the cache files located in ~/Library/Caches), the safest and most reliable tactic is simply to include everything. A file or folder that seems irrelevant to you may turn out to be crucial to the functioning of your system.

Archive Strategy

The archives you create should include all your important files (on each volume you use regularly, if you use more than one). The main question, though, is how you determine which files those are.

Some people suggest performing a full archive—that is, archiving every single file on your disk, just as you do when creating a duplicate. Others suggest performing a selective archive that includes only user-created data files, especially those that change frequently.

With a full archive, you have yet another copy of all your files besides your duplicates—an extra insurance policy. Restoring a full archive to an empty disk requires fewer steps, and less time, than restoring a selective archive (since in the latter case, you must restore a duplicate first). On the other hand, a full archive requires significantly more storage space, increasing your media cost, and takes longer to run. In addition, some backup software does not enable you to restore an archive as a bootable volume. My own preference is for selective archives, though I would not discourage you from performing a full archive if resources permit.

If you do choose to archive selectively, a good starting place is your home folder. By default, this folder contains most of your preference files, the files shown on your Desktop, and data for many of Apple's applications (Address Book, iCal, iTunes, iPhoto, Mail, Safari, and so on), among others. Although you can organize your hard disk however you want, Apple encourages you to keep all your user-created documents in the ~/Documents folder or elsewhere in your home folder. So it could be that all your important, user-specific data files exist somewhere inside your home folder—and if not, presumably you are aware of the locations of folders you've created elsewhere.

But even if you have assiduously colored within the lines and kept all your personal data in your home folder, should you archive the whole thing? In some cases, the answer is no.

Because Apple designed the home folder as a catch-all, it has the tendency to swell to enormous sizes. For example, if you maintain the default settings in iDVD, iMovie HD, iPhoto, and iTunes, all your digital media will be stored in your home folder. If, like me, you've imported your entire collection of CDs into iTunes, you may be looking at a huge Music folder (mine is well over 20 GB, and that is small compared to some). If you store digital video on your computer, your Movies folder will certainly be even larger.

Although there's nothing *wrong* with adding all those files to your archive, it may not be strictly necessary either—because all those files should already be backed up safely as part of the duplicates you maintain. If, as in the case of imported CD tracks, digital photos, or video downloads, you modify those folders less frequently than you perform duplicates, you might consider saving time and space by excluding them from archives. But if in doubt—especially when it comes to irreplaceable photos and video—err on the side of including them; having an extra backup just may save your bacon one day. Purchases from the iTunes Music Store also require special handling as I describe next.

Besides digital media, you may wish to manually exclude certain other files from an archive, if needed to save space. For instance:

Backing Up iTunes Music Store Purchases

Audio or video content you've purchased from the iTunes Music Store (iTMS) differs from music you've imported from CDs you own. Besides the fact that with downloaded files you don't have an original copy to serve as an extra backup, iTMS files include special copy protection to ensure that they can be played only by the purchaser, and only on one of up to five authorized computers. Because iTMS files are especially valuable, you should take extra steps to protect them:

◆ Always include iTMS tracks in your archive backups. If you import tracks from CDs as MP3 files, you can use your backup software's exclusion feature to filter out all MP3 files while keeping the AAC files (with an extension of .m4p) and MPEG-4 video files (with an extension of .m4v).

◆ Include the /Users/Shared folder in your archive backups as well; this folder contains hidden information required to enable authorization.

◆ If you suffer a severe crash and decide to erase your hard disk, deauthorize your computer before restoring from backup. (This prevents you from losing one of your five authorizations if your computer requires major repair.) Open iTunes and choose Advanced > Deauthorize Computer. Choose Deauthorize Computer for Apple Account, and click OK. After restoring your backup, open iTunes and choose Advanced > Authorize Computer.

- **Downloads:** Applications and other files you've downloaded from the Internet can nearly always be downloaded again. It may not be worth dedicating significant media space to hold such files.

- **Cache files:** Temporary cache files, such as those stored in ~/Library/ Caches, are not crucial to an archive, as they will be recreated automatically if needed.

Having determined what you need to back up and how often, you're ready to make decisions about what hardware you will need (see Chapter 10). If you decided earlier that you have special backup needs, though, continue on to read *Photo Backup Strategy*, next, or *Video and Audio Backup Strategy*, immediately thereafter.

Photo Backup Strategy

If you determined that your digital photos require special backup attention, consider these options in addition to (or, if you prefer, instead of) duplicates and archives.

Cataloging software

I have nothing at all against iPhoto—in fact, I quite like it. It even has the built-in capability of backing up your photos to optical discs (although it's a manual process). But iPhoto is a consumer-level application that wasn't designed for the needs of professionals—or amateurs who have tons of photos and take their images seriously. When your photo management needs outgrow iPhoto, you can move up to serious image-cataloging software.

For Mac OS X, you have two main choices: iView MediaPro (www.iview-multimedia.com; $160) and Extensis Portfolio (www.extensis.com; $200). Both have similar feature sets, including flexible searching, contact sheet creation, and much more. Crucially for our purposes, they maintain thumbnail catalogs of all your images even if you move the original files to another volume (and even if that volume happens to be sitting at the bottom of a pile of junk in your closet).

Note: Apple's Aperture application (`www.apple.com/aperture/`; $300) also contains cataloging and archiving tools for digital photos, though those are a small part of Aperture's capabilities, and it's overkill if you need just those features.

By using one of these applications to back up your photos (whether or not you delete the originals), you gain the ability to search a visual index for your images. When you find the one you want, the software will tell you which DVD, CD, or hard drive it's stored on.

On the downside, these third-party tools are more expensive than iPhoto, and not quite as easy to use; they also lack iPhoto's integration with applications such as Mail and iDVD. But these are minor complaints. For heavy-duty photo backups and cataloging, iView MediaPro and Extensis Portfolio can't be beat. (And if I had to choose between the two, I'd go with MediaPro: I prefer its interface and feature set—plus it's a bit less expensive.)

If you choose one of these tools, I suggest excluding photos from your regular archives and using the cataloging software's built-in backup tools for your photos instead. It'll be slightly more effort, but you'll dramatically increase the ease with which you can find and restore your photos. You can also, optionally, delete older photos from your hard disk after you've backed them up—you'll save room on your startup volume while still maintaining a handy catalog of thumbnails.

Photo-sharing services

If you're a .Mac member, you probably know that you can create Web pages to share your photos online. Of course, you pay for that privilege, and even with 1 GB of storage space, you may not have room for all your photos on your iDisk. Internet backup services (see *Internet Backup Services,* page 134) will gladly sell you more space on a server, but it doesn't come cheap—and such services won't enable you to share your photos on the Web.

Tip: For more detailed information about sharing your photos on the Web using iWeb, iPhoto, and .Mac HomePage, see my ebook *Take Control of .Mac* (www.takecontrolbooks.com/dot-mac.html)

Never fear, though: several companies provide *unlimited* storage for your digital photos, along with complete control over which ones are shared and with whom, for as little as zero dollars! (Yes, there's a catch, but it's surprisingly minor.)

Photo-sharing sites spring up all the time. Here are some of the more popular ones I knew of at the time I wrote this:

♦ **Flickr:** Free basic accounts limit monthly uploads to 20 MB of bandwidth usage and store only scaled-down images. Flickr Pro Accounts cost $25 per year and include a generous 2 GB monthly upload limit and unlimited storage of full-resolution images (www.flickr.com).

♦ **Fotki:** Free accounts give you 30 MB of space initially, and add 10 MB every 30 days. Premium accounts, which cost $50 per year, provide unlimited storage and a number of advanced features (www.fotki.com).

♦ **Kodak EasyShare Gallery:** Membership is free and includes unlimited storage, but with a catch: you must make a purchase of some kind (such as prints from your photos or other merchandise) at least once per year. Purchases need not be large, however, so if you're likely to purchase some prints anyway, it's effectively free (www.kodakgallery.com).

♦ **SmugMug:** Membership levels are Standard ($30 per year), Power User ($50 per year), and Pro ($100 per year). All levels include unlimited storage; higher levels provide more customization options and higher monthly traffic quotas (www.smugmug.com).

♦ **Snapfish:** Like the Kodak EasyShare Gallery, this service provides free, unlimited storage as long as you make at least one purchase annually (www.snapfish.com).

Except for Fotki, all these services offer Mac-compatible photo upload software; Fotki Premium members can upload photos via FTP.

Beyond the basics of photo storage and sharing, these sites differ in the range of features they offer. Most offer prints of your digital photos for a fee; some will send you CDs or DVDs with backups of your photos, too. And the range of additional services is varied and extensive; visit the sites and try their free trial memberships to get a feel for what they can do. (My favorite is SmugMug. The service is reasonably priced for unlimited storage, has the features I need, and offers upload software that integrates easily with iPhoto.)

Considering that you can back up *all* your photos for as little as a few dollars per year using one of these services, it's almost a no-brainer. In fact, even if you ignore all the other advice in this book, please take the easy step of backing up your photos with one of these services. And even if you already include your photos in your duplicates and archives, another off-site backup never hurts—and you'll get easy photo sharing as a bonus. The only people who might want to be circumspect about these services are those without broadband Internet connections: uploading photos over a slow connection can take a long, long time.

Tip: For more info on backing up your digital photos, see my article "Make your images last" in the August, 2005 issue of *Macworld:* www.macworld.com/2005/07/features/photosmanage/.

Video and Audio Backup Strategy

If you regularly edit video on your computer, you may need to adjust your backup strategy to account for the special requirements of these jumbo-sized files. (Although I speak of "video" throughout this section, keep in mind that essentially the same issues and strategies apply to pro audio files and other extra-large documents.)

Video data types

Think about the different forms video data may take:

◆ The original footage you shot with your camcorder—stored on whatever medium your camera uses: analog or digital tape (usually), or (occasionally) a DVD, built-in hard drive, or flash memory device.

◆ The raw files you transferred from the camcorder onto your computer's hard disk.

◆ A project (in, say, Final Cut Pro or iMovie HD) containing a particular selection of video files plus all the information about how they fit together—not to mention music, narration, titles, special effects, and so on. In the case of Final Cut Pro and Final Cut Express, this also includes video and audio cache files, which could be located on a separate connected hard disk.

◆ A final, rendered movie, in one or more sizes and formats (DVD-ready, Web-ready, etc.). Needless to say, a given project may be "final" and still undergo changes later!

Which of these items should you include in your backup plan—and how?

Original footage:
Let's begin with the tapes from your camcorder. The work you put into editing video clips into a finished product is valuable, but in most cases, the original footage is irreplaceable. However time-consuming or painful it may be, you could recreate a project from scratch, as long as you had a copy of the source material. So, when thinking about video backups, give special weight to that original footage.

Raw files on your hard disk:
If you've copied the data from your camcorder to your computer, you now have two copies. But not all your raw footage will end up as part of a movie; if you're like most people, you probably shoot a lot of extra material you'll never want to look at again. Those raw files—before they become part of an actual movie project—are generally the least important to back up (assuming, naturally, that you still have the originals).

Project files:

The project files are perhaps the most challenging component, because you may modify them many different times. If you include these files as part of a standard additive incremental archive, you may find (depending on which video editing and backup software you use, and several other variables) that even a tiny change to a 20 GB video project results in the *entire* 20 GB file being *added* to each day's archive. If you happen to have a few terabyte or larger drives sitting around, that's not much of a problem, but such drives are still on the expensive side for most of us.

Archives of your project files can be worthwhile, but such archives generally benefit work in progress more than older material. In other words, once you've completed this year's holiday DVD and sent it off to your family, you're unlikely to need all the intermediate versions of the project files again—though you may want the final project files later on.

Final, rendered movies:

As for the final product, it goes without saying that it's important, but as long as you still have the project files, you can recreate it if necessary. So it's a bit less crucial to back up than your project files.

Recommendations

Although I can't offer a one-size-fits all approach to video backups, I would like to make some recommendations that you can tailor to your specific situation. All these suggestions presume that you're already making duplicates and archives of your non-video data:

♦ Exclude video data from your regular archives and duplicates. That'll make those backups more manageable, saving both time and media.

♦ Assuming your camcorder stores its data on removable media, *always* keep the original media—don't overwrite it for your next project, even though you've copied the data to your computer. Instead, treat that tape, DVD, or cartridge as though it were a film negative and store it in a safe place. You'll use up more media this way, but you'll have an automatic backup of all your footage.

♦ Consider making a duplicate of each piece of original media (if your video equipment provides a way to do so). Remember, every piece of backup media is subject to deterioration over time, so an extra copy is never a bad idea.

♦ You probably do *not* need to back up video data that you've copied from your camera to your hard disk but are not actively using. (After all, you already have one or two backups of this data in the form of your original tapes and, perhaps, duplicates of them.)

♦ As for your active video projects, at minimum, you should use your backup software to copy them onto an external hard drive and update that copy periodically. Better still, set up an archive of your active video data—separate from your regular data—on a hard drive. This will give you at least a few intermediate versions of your work in progress, should you need to go back to an earlier one. (How often you update this archive will depend on your available disk space.)

♦ When you've finished a project and know you won't be editing it again in the near future, copy all your project files onto optical media—preferably, two or more sets that you'll store in separate places. Then delete the project files from your hard disk and recycle your video archive disk by erasing and starting over again with a full backup of your next project.

♦ If your finished product is a DVD, be sure to save an extra copy of that DVD as a backup. For movies in other formats, consider copying them manually onto optical discs for long-term storage.

Tip: Don't be tempted to think that your final DVD project is also a backup. DVD video is compressed with MPEG-2 encoding, which means the DVD you watch on television contains video at a lower quality than what you edited. If you need to go back and re-edit it, the results won't be as good as if you used the original source material from the camcorder or hard disk. Plus, you can't easily pull video from a DVD disc; you need special conversion software.

In other words, treat your video data with the same care you give all your other files, but don't get hung up on long-term storage of every single edit you make. The most important things to back up are your original footage, archives of work currently in progress, and your final project files.

Windows Files Backup Strategy

Now that Apple offers Boot Camp software for Intel Macs, more and more people are installing Windows XP in its own partition. Meanwhile, virtualization software (such as Parallels Desktop and Q) is also catching on, as it enables users to run Windows at *nearly* full speed alongside Mac OS X without rebooting.

Needless to say, if you're running Windows on your Mac, you should back up your Windows files too. When you do, keep the following tips in mind:

♦ The Windows partition Boot Camp creates is, as far as Mac OS X is concerned, just another volume. So any Mac backup software you use can access its files (in whole or in part) the same way as your Mac files. However…

♦ When you reboot your computer into Windows using Boot Camp, your Mac software can't run. If you reboot regularly in Mac OS X, you can let your Mac backup software handle your Windows files then. But if you do extensive work in Windows and don't switch back to Mac OS X for days at a time, consider installing Windows backup software instead.

♦ If you use virtualization software such as Parallels Desktop, Q, Virtual PC, or GuestPC, your Windows files will live in a special disk image that appears as a regular volume within Windows. Mac backup software can't see inside that image to back up individual files, and simply running Windows will modify the image file—meaning your backup program will consider the whole file to have changed. You can, of course, copy that entire image, but it may be quite large. As with FileVault images (see the sidebar *FileVault and Backups,* page 168), adding these disk images to your archives will rapidly chew up your disk space. Therefore, consider backing these images up separately (and less frequently than your other archives).

Alternatively, run Windows backup software within your virtual machine to back up your Windows files separately or, better yet, install a Windows *client* for backup software (such as Retrospect Desktop) running in Mac OS X, and treat the Windows virtual machine as a network client.

10 Choose Your Backup Hardware

I remember vividly the days of backing up my hard disk onto a tall stack of floppies. Back when a 40 MB drive was standard, I would have been thrilled to think I could put 16 or more copies of my disk on a single CD-R. A few years later, conventional wisdom held that DAT (digital audio tape) drives were the way to go for many power users. Now, however, with hard disk sizes routinely reaching 400 GB, we have to reconsider old notions about backup hardware and media. You probably have a lot of data to copy, and the amount will only increase. But you don't want to spend a fortune on your backup system, and you don't want backups to take all day. What to do?

Although floppy disks are effectively dead, optical drives (to burn CDs and DVDs), tape drives, Zip and Jaz drives, and the like are still common, and since you may have these already, you will certainly want to consider the pros and cons of using them for backups. Hard drives are much less expensive than they once were, and for many people make the ideal backup device. There's also the possibility of backing up to a network server of one kind or another—and even your camcorder. In this section, I sort through all the major hardware options and help you to decide which is best for your backups.

Hard Drives

Let me begin with my favorite option: hard drives. I use and suggest hard drives as a backup medium, and in almost every case I strongly believe they're the best choice for individuals and small networks. If you can possibly manage it, you will achieve Maximum Backup Happiness by using external hard drives.

Note: I deliberately said *external* hard drives—even though you could save some money on the enclosures and extra electronics by buying drives that can be mounted inside your desktop Power Mac. I advocate external drives because:

♦ You can disconnect an external drive and store it off-site—an important safeguard against theft.

♦ If your computer suffers severe damage due to a power surge, a leaky roof, or being knocked off the desk accidentally, your internal hard drives may fail along with the rest of the machine.

Hard Drive Virtues

I suspect that your initial impulse, like mine, is to cringe at the cost of external hard drives—especially since, as I explained earlier, you should have at least two, and perhaps three of them. They may seem extravagant in a way that DVD-Rs, say, do not. So let me sing the praises of hard drives for a moment, while at the same time explaining why they're not only the best solution, they're economical too. Here's what makes hard drives great:

♦ **Speed:** The first thing hard drives have going for them is speed. You may have tens or hundreds of gigabytes of data on your computer's internal hard disk. But copying such large amounts of data can be extraordinarily time-consuming under the best of circumstances. Even fast optical drives and tape drives generally transfer data at a fraction of the speed of a slow hard drive. If you want to do more with your computer than watch it back up your data, you'll appreciate the time savings a hard drive provides.

♦ **Capacity:** If you're backing up to a medium with less capacity than your hard disk, sooner or later you'll have to swap media. Even the newest double-layer DVDs can't store the entire contents of a moderately large hard disk on a single disc. Swapping media isn't the worst thing in the world, but the more often you have to do so, the more of an aggravation backing up becomes. If, on the other hand, you use an external hard drive with sufficient capacity, you'll never have to swap media—and you can allow your backups to run unattended at any time of the day or night.

Warning! Backing Up to Another Partition: If you have a nice, large internal hard disk and far too little data to fill it, you may be tempted to partition it into several volumes and store backups on each one—instead of using separate physical drives. Although this is marginally better than not backing up at all, it's still an incredibly bad idea. Hard drives usually don't die one partition at a time. You could easily encounter a problem that makes it impossible to access any part of the disk, in which case your backups would be of no use. And just like a second internal drive, a second partition is vulnerable to theft and damage that affects your entire computer.

♦ **Random access:** In addition to raw speed in copying files, hard drives offer the enormous advantage of random access. Besides using space more efficiently, this means that it takes no longer to restore files recorded over a period of weeks than it does to restore files recorded on a single date.

♦ **Versatility:** When you use a hard drive for backups, you can put both duplicates and archives on the same device. You can (usually) boot from it, and even, in a pinch, use it as supplemental storage for other projects. Perhaps more importantly, using a hard drive keeps your optical drive (or other removable storage devices) free for installing software, burning DVDs, or other day-to-day tasks.

♦ **Economy:** As I write this, 250 GB FireWire drives can be found at retail for well under $200, and if you look online at discount stores and eBay auctions, you can find them for even less. That's quite a bargain—especially when you factor in the recurring costs of optical media or tapes. Further, how much is your time worth? Can you afford to spend an entire day restoring from a stack of CD-ROMs? If, instead, you could be up and running minutes after a drive failure, what would that be worth to you? Based on my own experience, I can say with conviction that an initial investment of a few hundred dollars pays for itself many times over when you consider the time and aggravation it saves in the long run.

Does Size Matter?

If you're using a hard drive for backups, how large does it need to be? This seemingly tricky question has a relatively easy answer: as a rule of thumb, a destination volume should have between 1 and 1.5 times the capacity of the source volume. Sometimes one can comfortably store both a duplicate and several months' worth of an archive on a single disk the same size as the one being backed up—but you can check this with a little bit of math.

I advocate partitioning each backup disk into two volumes—one for a duplicate and one for archives (see *Partition Hard Disks,* page 160). It's easy to figure out how much space you need for each, and then add the two amounts together to get a total disk size for the backup drive.

For duplicates, you need a volume that will hold all the data on your hard disk—which may be much smaller than its actual capacity—and provide some extra breathing room. To find out how much space your data

Hard Drives and Long-Term Storage

According to conventional wisdom, hard drives are a poor choice for *long-term* data storage. Exactly how long "long" is can be debated. If you believe manufacturers' specifications for mean time between failures (MTBF), the typical drive should run continuously for at least 10 years before failing. However, the magnetic particles coating the platters are likely to randomly lose their charges much sooner than that, and many other causes of hard drive misbehavior don't technically count as "failure" as far as the manufacturer is concerned.

Data corruption can occur at any time, but my confidence in a hard drive begins to deteriorate after about 3 years, and after 5 years or so, I no longer consider it a safe bet for backup data storage.

You could have a hard drive that behaves perfectly for decades, but the odds are against you. As a practical matter, I suggest factoring in the purchase of new backup drives when you buy a new Mac—or every 2 to 3 years, whichever is more often.

currently occupies, select your hard drive's icon in the Finder and choose File > Get Info. The figure next to the word "Used" (**Figure 13**) is the amount of space the data currently occupies.

Figure 13

The Finder's Get Info window for a hard disk. The number next to "Used" indicates the amount of data currently stored on the volume.

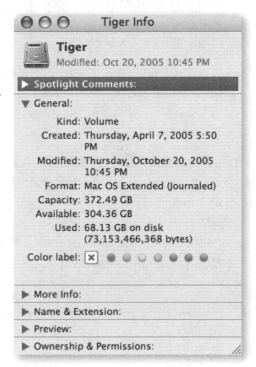

Assuming that you regularly add new files to your computer, you will want to leave yourself a significant cushion—make the volume for the duplicate enough larger to hold the files you're likely to add during the next six to twelve months. If you do not have a good sense of the rate at which your data will grow, multiply the Used figure by 1.5, and then round up to the nearest gigabyte. (In this example, the volume "Tiger" would require at least 103 GB for a duplicate.) In any case, there's never a need for your duplicate volume to be larger than the total capacity of the disk you're backing up.

For archives, the situation is slightly different: on the one hand, your backup software may compress your data, decreasing the space used; on the other, you will continually add new and modified files, increasing the space used.

Begin by determining the total space occupied by the data you plan to archive (again, use the Finder's Get Info command), which could be your entire disk if you perform a full archive, or perhaps only your home folder and a few other items if you perform a selective archive. Next, subtract the total size of any subfolders you intend to exclude (for example, ~/Music/iTunes/iTunes Music).

Now multiply this total by 1.5. The resulting figure—let's call it x—is the minimum amount of space you should allot for an archive partition if you're using compression. Without compression, multiply x by two.

Note: If you're backing up several computers over a network to a single set of media, be sure to perform these calculations for each computer, and then add them together. Although some network backup software (including Retrospect) can save space by maintaining just one copy of a file that's identical across multiple computers, you'll be safer if you ignore that possibility and allow more breathing room.

I hasten to point out that these figures represent recommended *minimums*. They will enable you to back up your data comfortably today; but as your hard disk fills up, you want a backup disk that can keep up with it. So all things considered, you should buy a backup disk no smaller than your source disk.

It could be, for instance, that on a 60 GB hard disk, you currently have 20 GB of data in total, of which your home folder, not counting excluded files, is only 6 GB. If you allow 30 GB (20 GB x 1.5) for a duplicate and 9 GB (6 GB x 1.5) for an archive, that yields 39 GB. Resist the temptation to save money by purchasing a 40 GB disk, because sooner or later, you're likely to fill up that internal disk and wish you had more backup space. You know the saying: you can never have too much money or disk space. Buy a 60 GB disk—or, if you can afford it, an 80 GB disk.

Why not 120 GB? Or 250 GB? Why not buy the biggest disks you can afford? There's nothing wrong with getting a bigger disk, but after about 1.5 times the capacity of your internal disk, you reach a point of diminishing returns—by the time you fill it completely (assuming a compressed archive), the drive will be too old to depend on.

Likewise, you may be thinking that if you bought a larger disk than necessary, you could use the extra space for other data. But I strongly encourage you to use a backup drive exclusively for backups. Otherwise you may be tempted to keep the backup drives hooked up instead of storing them more safely.

Choosing a Hard Drive

Because so many different external hard drives exist, the choice can be daunting. Here's my quick guide to what you need to know:

◆ **Interface:** All things being equal, get a drive with the fastest interface your computer supports. (FireWire 800 and USB 2.0 are faster than FireWire 400, which is much faster than USB 1.1; with add-in cards, you can get even faster interfaces than FireWire 800, such as Ultra 320 SCSI, Fibre Channel, SATA (Serial ATA), and SATA II. However, be aware that not all add-in cards enable you to boot from external drives; if

USB 2.0 Drives, Intel Macs, and Bootability

Almost every Mac with a FireWire port can boot from an external FireWire drive (either the 400 or 800 variety). However, only Intel-based Macs can boot into Mac OS X from USB 2.0 hard drives. Therefore, if you're looking for a drive on which to store duplicates, I suggest choosing either FireWire-only or combination FireWire/USB hard drives, which will give you the broadest compatibility.

However, be aware of two important points regarding Intel Macs:

◆ Despite Apple's claims to the contrary, Intel Macs *can* boot from hard disks formatted using the Apple Partition Map (APM) scheme, which has been the norm on PowerPC-based Macs for years. The catch is that currently, the Tiger *installer* refuses to recognize such disks as a valid destination and instead requires you to reformat the drives with Disk Utility to use the new GUID Partition Table (GPT) scheme. Luckily, however, you don't need to worry about any of this when making backups. If you use one of the utilities described in this book to create a duplicate from your Intel Mac, it will be bootable even if the volume uses APM.

◆ If you have an Intel Mac with any version of Tiger (10.4) on it and make a duplicate of your startup volume, that volume will *not* boot a PowerPC-based Mac; likewise, a duplicate of a PowerPC-based Mac's Tiger startup volume will not boot an Intel Mac. Apple is expected to eliminate this inconvenience with the release of Mac OS X 10.5 Leopard, which should be a universal system that will boot Macs with either type of processor.

in doubt, check with the manufacturer before purchasing the card.) Up to a point, a faster interface typically translates into quicker back-ups—though in real-world use, FireWire 800 is usually not appreciably faster than FireWire 400. Many modern drives offer combinations of two or more of these interfaces.

♦ **One-touch backups:** Maxtor sells OneTouch external hard drives with a button that enables you to launch software and execute a backup just by pressing it (www.maxtor.com). Seagate offers something similar, the Pushbutton Back-up Hard Drive (www.seagate.com). IOGEAR ups the ante on their Tri-Select ION drives, which feature three buttons (each of which can run a different backup script; www.iogear.com). I'd rather have my backups run on a schedule—one less button to press! However, the Maxtor and IOGEAR drives include a free copy of Retrospect Express, so they're worth a few dollars extra. (The Seagate drives include a copy of CMS BounceBack Express, a limited version of the BounceBack Professional duplication software.) You can ignore the button(s)—or, if you prefer, set a button to run your Duplicate or Archive script and press it to make an instant backup after you've made especially important changes.

♦ **Automatic backups:** CMS Products' ABSplus drives include soft-ware that performs a duplicate as soon as you plug in the drive (www.cmsproducts.com). That's great—but only part of what we want. I'd opt instead for the flexibility of standard backup software. Feel free to get an ABSplus, but plan to supply your own software, at least for archiving.

♦ **Build-your-own:** Numerous companies sell FireWire- or USB-equipped cases into which you can place your own IDE drive mechanism. If you're comfortable doing some minor tinkering and bargain hunting, you may be able to save a bit of money this way. Be aware, however, that some older cases cannot accommodate disks over 120 GB; check the manufacturer's specifications before making a purchase.

♦ **Hot-swappable assemblies:** Granite Digital (www.granitedigital.com) and WiebeTech (www.wiebetech.com) sell hot-swappable FireWire hard drive assemblies. You get a single case, power supply, and cable, to which you add one or more hard drives, each in its own special carrier tray. You can pop out one hard drive and pop in another quickly, making it quite easy to rotate backup sets—no messing with cables. I've used Granite drives and they're certainly nice, but you pay quite a premium for what amounts to a small added convenience.

♦ **Multi-drive enclosures:** Another new trend in external hard drives is enclosures containing two or more drive mechanisms (whether individually removable or not) that you can configure, using included software, as a RAID (see the sidebar *Can a RAID Substitute for Duplicates?*, page 92). Examples are Maxtor's OneTouch III, Turbo Edition (which also, naturally, features the one-touch backup feature mentioned just previously; www.maxtor.com) and LaCie's Two Big device (which uses a SATA II interface; www.lacie.com). Such drives can provide either redundancy for your backups (if configured as a mirrored RAID) or additional speed (if configured as a striped RAID). Although I can think of many excellent uses for these devices, they may be overkill for backups; I think most people would be better served by having two physically separate drive units than one enclosure with two mechanisms.

♦ **Encrypted hard drives:** One problem with putting a bootable duplicate on an external hard drive is that you can't use your backup software's encryption feature; if the files have to be decrypted by software before the system can read them, you won't be able to boot from that drive. (And thus, ordinarily, only archives can be encrypted.) This isn't much of a worry unless, as I recommend, you store one of your backup drives offsite at all times—if someone else gets their hands on it, they have immediate access to all your data. The solution is to use a drive that features *hardware* encryption, meaning everything written to the drive is encrypted automatically, and everything read from the drive is decrypted automatically, by circuitry in the drive enclosure; instead of typing in a password, you secure the data using a physical electronic key. (Needless to say, you will have to keep that key in a very safe place, separate from the drive itself!) Several manufacturers now make such drives (or enclosures to which you can add your own drive). They're more expensive, but an excellent investment if you store sensitive personal data on your drives. Examples include RocStor's Rocbit drives (www.rocsecure.com) and RadTech's Impact enclosures (www.radtech.us/Products/Impact.aspx).

- **iPods:** You can use your iPod as a backup device if it has enough free space—but remember, that will limit the number of songs and photos you can store. (Bear in mind that only older iPods with FireWire interfaces can be used as startup disks for PowerPC-based Macs.) iPods are also more vulnerable to theft, since you're more likely to carry them around with you—so be sure your backups are encrypted!

- **Brands and warranties:** Although hard drives are in some ways commodity items, you'll still pay more for a brand name than a generic drive. Is the extra money worth it? Often not. The drive mechanisms themselves come from relatively few manufacturers, all of which are quite reputable—it's the cases, power supplies, and supporting electronics that vary from vendor to vendor. Look for a one-year or better warranty, and check out the manufacturer's Web site to look for signs of life and Mac support. But don't be afraid of second-tier brands. (For instance, I have a pair of FireWire drives from Buslink—a brand that doesn't even claim Mac compatibility—that have served me flawlessly for years, even though I bought them dirt cheap on eBay.)

Tip: You can often find bargains on hard drives from a wide range of manufacturers and dealers at dealmac (`www.dealmac.com`). Drive prices are constantly dropping, and special offers and rebates appear frequently. If you're looking for a particular type or capacity of drive, consider signing up for dealmac's watch list—you'll get an email alert when a deal matching your criteria appears.

One additional note: If you end up with more FireWire devices than your Mac has FireWire ports, consider picking up an inexpensive FireWire hub rather than daisy-chaining drives together. A hub gives you the ability to connect or disconnect any drive without affecting the others.

Optical Media

The various flavors of recordable CDs and DVDs are collectively known as *optical media,* because they rely on lasers to read and write data to them. Most of the Macs made in the past several years include a *SuperDrive,* which can write to and read from DVD media (4.7 GB) and CD media (up to 800 MB); some have *Combo drives* that can read from DVDs and write to CDs.

Apple is constantly upgrading the capabilities of the optical drives in their computers. Starting in mid-2005, some Macs included SuperDrives that could read and write to double-layer (8.5 GB) DVD+R discs. In the future, DVD varieties with even greater capacity—such as Blu-ray and HD-DVD— will become common, and will probably find their way into new Macs. See **Table 2** for an overview of current optical media types.

Table 2: Optical Media Types				
Name	**Capacity**	**Rewritable?**	**Use with Combo Drive**	**Use with SuperDrive**
CD-ROM	up to 800 MB	No	Read-only	Read-only
CD-R	650, 700, or 800 MB	No	Yes	Yes
CD-RW	650, 700, or 800 MB	Yes	Yes	Yes
DVD-ROM	up to 4.7 GB	No	Read-only	Read-only
DVD-R	4.7 GB	No	Read-only	Yes
DVD-RW	4.7 GB	Yes	Read-only	[1]
DVD+R	4.7 GB	No	No	[2]
DVD+RW	4.7 GB	Yes	No	[2]
DVD+R DL (double-layer)	8.5 GB	No	No	[3]
DVD-RAM	up to 9.4 GB	Yes	No	No

[1] Except on very early SuperDrive models. Although the Finder does not support DVD-RW media on older SuperDrives, some third-party software may.

[2] All SuperDrives shipped in 2005 and later included DVD+R and DVD+RW support.

[3] In 2005, Apple added DVD+R DL support to SuperDrives in the Power Mac, iMac, eMac, and PowerBook lines. Intel-based Mac mini models and some MacBook Pro models also include SuperDrives that can write to double-layer DVDs. Apple may add this capability to other models in the future.

Because built-in optical drives do not require an additional purchase (except the media, which is relatively inexpensive), it's logical to consider using them for backups. In a few cases they may be adequate, but in general I'd like to steer you away from backing up your Mac onto optical media.

The first thing I should point out is that backing up to any optical media is *slow.* If you have only a few gigabytes of data to back up, this may not bother you, but as your storage needs increase, you're more likely to find it problematic. True enough, some optical drives are faster than others; a 52x CD burner will obviously require much less of your time than a 2x burner. Even so, the fastest optical drives transfer data at less than one-tenth the speed of the slowest hard drives. And if you're talking about backing up many gigabytes of data, you're still looking at an extremely lengthy process.

Tip: Not sure which kinds of media your Mac's optical drive can record on? Open Terminal (in /Applications/Utilities) and enter:

`drutil info`

A list of supported media types will appear after the label CD-Write (for CD formats) and DVD-Write (for DVD formats). (In this list, "DL" stands for double-layer.)

Another disadvantage of using your optical drive for backups is that it requires your attention. If your backups run automatically on a schedule, you must make sure a blank disc is in the recorder at the proper time. If you schedule backups for when you're using the Mac (so that you can easily swap discs), you face the possibility that you'll want to use your optical drive for some other reason—and even if not, your Mac may slow down unacceptably during the backup process.

Financial considerations alone make optical media an attractive option, despite their disadvantages. But before you decide on an optical drive as your backup device, consider the following factors.

Recordable CDs

CDs (including CD-R and CD-RW) make a poor choice for duplicating your entire hard drive. The highest-capacity CDs you can buy—which, by the way, may or may not be compatible with your hardware and software—hold 800 MB. (Standard CDs hold either 650 or 700 MB.) In order to duplicate your entire hard disk—even with the smallest possible installation of Tiger—you would need four to six discs, depending on their capacity. And if you want to duplicate a full 120 GB hard disk, that will require upwards of 170 discs! Even then, you will not be able to boot from your duplicate; you'd need to restore it to a hard disk first. Because of the number of discs required, the amount of user interaction the backup will require, and the inability to boot from the final product, CDs are a bad idea for duplicates.

When it comes to archive backups, CDs show a bit more promise. Yes, it still takes a stack of them, and yes, that means time-consuming sessions of swapping (and labeling!) discs. However, if you're backing up only your data files (not your entire hard disk)—and particularly after your first session, when you're incrementally backing up only changed files—the time and aggravation it requires will be much less. As CDs go, CD-RW media has an edge over CD-R (even though it's almost twice as expensive) in that it can be erased and reused when your stack of discs becomes too large (see *Recycling vs. Long-Term Archives*, page 172).

Recordable DVDs

Recordable DVDs may all look alike, but they vary in format and capacity. (See **Table 2**, page 125, for an overview of the different formats.) Early Apple SuperDrives supported only DVD-R media, though with the right software, you could also use erasable DVD-RW media. A pair of competing standards—DVD+R and DVD+RW—is supported by currently shipping SuperDrives and most third-party external DVD recorders. In addition, newer third-party drives—and SuperDrives in most Macs shipped from mid-2005 on—can use double-layer DVD+R media with a capacity of 8.5 GB (a single-layer DVD can hold up to 4.7 GB).

Note: You will sometimes see drives described as supporting "DVD±R" or "DVD±RW." The ± symbol means both + and – (as in, DVD+R *and* DVD-R). And if a drive supports a rewriteable format, it also supports the corresponding write-only format. So, for example, a DVD±RW drive also supports DVD-R and DVD+R.

Another standard, known as DVD-RAM, is also supported by many third-party drives (as well as some older Macs). Depending on the format, a DVD-RAM disc can hold up to 9.4 GB of data.

Despite these differences, recordable DVDs all share the same basic traits: significantly higher capacities than CDs, offset by much slower recording speeds.

First, the good news: if you want the lowest possible cost per gigabyte of storage over the long run, you can hardly do better than DVD-RW (or DVD+RW) discs—if your optical drive and software supports them. Buy a package of 50 (typically sold without cases on a plastic spindle) for under $50, and you have enough media to back up a medium-sized hard disk for a couple of years. When all the discs are full, erase them and start again. DVD-R discs, although not erasable, are a bit cheaper than rewritable DVD-RW or DVD+RW media, and will work with any SuperDrive. DVD+R DL discs hold more data, but are not erasable.

But there's a catch—several catches, in fact:

♦ Even the highest-capacity recordable DVDs may not be able to store the entire contents of your hard disk.

♦ In cases where you can duplicate your entire hard disk onto a DVD, you will still, in general, be unable to boot from the DVD. As with CDs, you must restore the duplicate onto a hard disk first.

♦ Erasing rewritable DVDs (DVD-RW and DVD+RW) can be rather time-consuming.

Final Thoughts on Optical Drives

I believe the best backup strategy requires the least manual effort. Because optical media tend to require a lot of manual effort—and because they do not provide you with a bootable backup—they're less than ideal. However, if you've just spent your entire savings on a new iMac and you can't possibly spring for even a single external hard drive, backing up onto optical media is vastly better than not backing up at all. Just keep these thoughts in mind:

♦ For minimum inconvenience, use the highest-capacity discs your drive supports (i.e., DVD rather than CD).

♦ If saving money is paramount, use rewritable media (DVD-RW or DVD+RW), if your drive and software support it.

♦ Because incremental duplicates are impossible with optical media, plan on making a duplicate just once a month.

Magneto-Optical Disks

Several different manufacturers offer magneto-optical (MO) drives and disks, ranging in capacity from 128 MB to 9.1 GB. Some of these are write-once like CD-Rs (the acronym WORM, for Write Once, Read Many, applies to such disks and drives); others are rewritable like CD-RWs and can be erased. The primary advantage of MO technology over CDs and DVDs is longevity: MO media is typically rated for long-term archival storage on the order of 100 years. On the other hand, MO media is extremely expensive, as are the drives themselves. The mechanisms are considerably slower than conventional optical drives. And MO media comes in many different formats and sizes—once you choose a media type, your future options may be limited.

The latest development in MO is called UDO (Ultra-Density Optical), with disks that can hold as much as 30 GB each. If regular MO drives and media are expensive, UDO is out of this world: plan on spending about $4000 for a low-end drive, plus upwards of $60 for a single rewritable cartridge.

Because the backup plan I'm recommending here does not require extremely long-term storage of media, and because I assume you do not wish to spend more on your backup device and media than what you paid for your Mac, I see no reason to consider MO or UDO drives.

Other Removable Media

Besides optical discs and magneto-optical disks, you can find many other removable storage devices, from a wide range of manufacturers. The most popular ones—and, for our purposes, the only ones potentially worth considering—are made by Iomega.

Iomega Zip and Jaz

Iomega Zip drives store 100 MB to 750 MB on removable magnetic disk cartridges that are slower than hard drives, but usually faster than optical discs and much faster than tape drives. Although the cost of media per gigabyte is comparatively high, Zip disks can be reused indefinitely. The same is true of the now-discontinued Jaz drives, which support 1 GB and 2 GB Jaz disks. Unfortunately, Zip and Jaz disks have a reputation for being unreliable, so I recommend against using them for backups.

Iomega REV

Iomega's latest removable-storage device, REV, uses rugged, hard disk-based cartridges that hold 35 GB each (www.iomega.com). Designed as a faster and more robust backup platform than tapes or DVDs, the FireWire version of this drive even includes a free copy of Retrospect Express. Although REV is significantly slower than ordinary hard drives, the cost of a single drive (about $300) plus several disks (about $50 each) could be less than the cost of two or more stand-alone hard drives.

The only significant downside is that 35 GB is not large enough to hold the contents of some users' startup volumes; although you can certainly split a backup onto multiple disks, this would prevent you from making a bootable duplicate. However, if you have well under 35 GB of data on your startup volume, REV may be an excellent choice. A word of caution: REV is a recent and relatively untested technology. Given the poor reputation of Zip and Jaz drives, it might be wise to wait for evidence of reliability before trusting your data to REV.

Tape Drives

For many years, digital tape drives were considered the only reasonable, cost-effective way to back up large quantities of data. They're still extremely popular in large businesses. Common digital tape formats include VXA and DDS (a data-optimized variant of DAT, digital audio tape). Although at one time tapes were notorious for losing data spontaneously, they have now achieved a comfortably high level of reliability and longevity. And in (extremely large) quantity, they can be quite economical—though most of us will never get to the point where that economy of scale kicks in.

Tape drives have many virtues, but speed is not one of them—at least, not for the lower-end tape drive most of us mere mortals can afford. It takes far longer to back up a given amount of data to a tape than to even a slow optical disk. Restoring files is even more time-consuming, because tapes must be rewound or fast-forwarded to the correct spot before the data can be transferred. And you will never be able to boot your Mac from a tape drive.

When truly phenomenal quantities of data must be backed up, when money is no object, and when time is plentiful, tape drives are perfect.

A Reminder about Redundancy

As I suggested earlier in *Keeping Multiple Backups* (page 98), no matter which type of backup medium you use, you should always keep multiple copies of your backups. That means multiple hard drives or multiple sets of removable media (of whichever sort). There's always the chance that a single backup will suffer the same fate as your hard drive: a random failure of some sort. If you attempt to restore files from a backup and find that it's damaged, you'll be grateful that you had a spare copy.

Better yet, if possible, consider maintaining *three* sets of backups, one of which is kept at a separate location from your computer at all times. I discuss off-site backups in more detail later under *Mind Your Media* (page 172). Although an off-site backup is possible even if you have only two sets, having three makes it much more convenient.

High-capacity tape libraries—automated systems that can robotically swap tapes into and out of a bank of tape drives—are marvelous (and marvelously expensive) toys that form the backbone of many corporate backup systems. But for ordinary people with modest amounts of data, too little time, and even less money, they make little sense. Consider that you may spend about $1600 for a drive that supports 80 GB tapes, which in turn cost about $80 each. For that price, you could buy sixteen 80 GB hard drives or four 500 GB hard drives, which should be enough to provide speedy, redundant backups for all but the most extreme Mac setups.

Flash Drives

Flash drives, those small, solid-state, keychain-sized gizmos you plug into a USB port and use to shuttle files around, are all the rage these days. Because they're compact, have no moving parts, and can store, in some cases, as much data as three CDs, you may think they're a good backup medium. And for quick, one-off backups of files you're actively working on, they're not bad. At some hypothetical future date when you can buy, say, a 60 GB flash drive for little more than a hard drive, they may be useful for full backups too. For now, though, they are too small to store a complete, bootable Mac OS X system, and compared to any other medium available, the cost per gigabyte for archive backups is absurdly high.

SAN and NAS

Another trendy buzzword in data storage is *SAN*, or *storage area network*. A SAN is nothing more than one or more hard drives able to be shared among several computers, generally via high-speed FireWire, Fibre Channel, or SCSI connections (without using a conventional Ethernet-based network). *NAS*, or *network attached storage*, typically refers to one or more hard drives with their own Ethernet (or wireless) interfaces, sort of minimalist file servers. (Increasingly, they're simply called "network drives.") In other words, SAN and NAS equipment may be nearly identical, except for their interfaces.

Your office may have a SAN or NAS system available, and if enough adequate free space is available to you, there's nothing wrong with using either for backups. However, I would not buy SAN or NAS products primarily for home or small-office backup use. When it comes to backups, they provide little or no benefit over conventional FireWire or USB hard drives. And because they can't run backup software themselves, you still have to set up a backup server—or have each machine run its own backup application.

Also, bear in mind that it may not be possible to boot your machine directly from a duplicate stored on a SAN or NAS device; in general, you will have to restore (or re-duplicate) a duplicate to another hard drive first. And although some SAN or NAS setups may offer terrific speed and capacity for frequent backups, transporting a set of media off-site (or back when a restore is needed) is likely to be difficult or impossible.

Local Network Servers

If, in your home or office, a computer is functioning as a file server, it's certainly worth considering whether you could use a network volume (AFP, SMB, or otherwise) as a backup destination.

In general, if you have control over the server yourself, I recommend adding a separate physical hard drive and installing client-server backup software. Otherwise, your backups will be commingled with other files, making it difficult to store them off-site and potentially creating a security risk.

If you do not personally have control over the server (i.e., if it's a shared company server), be circumspect about using it for backups. You could easily use up more space than you should, and you risk incurring the wrath of your IT manager. Even if she's willing to give you your own capacious partition on a server hard disk, you'll have much less flexibility and control over your data than if you backed it up to local media.

iDisk

Subscribers to Apple's .Mac service (at $100 per year) currently get up to 1 GB of iDisk storage space, with the option to increase to 2 GB for $50 per year or 4 GB for $100 per year. Apple's Backup application, and most other backup utilities, can use an iDisk as a backup destination. Unfortunately, even 2 GB is far too little space to meet most users' needs, and transfer speeds to the .Mac servers are often quite slow, even for users with broadband connections. In addition, you cannot make a bootable backup onto an iDisk. For these reasons, your iDisk is not an ideal backup destination.

On the other hand, for casual (manual or automatic) backups of just a few files between regularly scheduled archives, an iDisk does make a convenient—and inherently off-site—destination.

Internet Backup Services

A few years ago, during the dot-com boom, Internet backup services were hailed as the next big thing. The idea is simple: using either a conventional backup program such as Retrospect or proprietary software, perform backups as usual, but use secure Internet file servers—rather than local or network volumes—as the destination. In other words, an Internet backup service is basically a more-sophisticated version of using Apple Backup with your iDisk.

In theory, I like the idea of remote Internet backup. In fact, I used such a service for a while—until it went out of business. The problem was that the cost of doing this type of business was out of proportion to the amount of money most consumers could be expected to pay.

Only a handful of Mac-compatible Internet backup services remain, and they are still quite pricey, especially compared to the cost of purchasing your own hard drives. Here are the ones I'm aware of:

♦ **BackJack:** BackJack (*www.backjack.com*) charges $12.50 per month for 2 GB of storage space, with additional space available at $2.75 per gigabyte (the per-gigabyte cost decreases as you add storage). An alternate plan, which includes extra, redundant backups, costs $17.50 per month for 2 GB and $6.00 per additional gigabyte (again, with cost reductions as you add storage).

♦ **Tuloy:** Tuloy (www.tuloy.com) charges $3.95 per month for 500 MB of storage, their maximum.

♦ **Prolifix:** Prolifix (www.prolifix.net) uses cross-platform, Java-based software. The company charges $9.95 per month for 500 MB of storage and $28.95 per month for 8 GB, with intermediate levels available. (Contact Prolifix for quotes on higher storage quotas.)

♦ **Datatrieve:** Located in the U.K., Datatrieve uses a Java-based client (www.datatrieve.co.uk). They charge £5 (about $9) per month for 1 GB of storage, and £64 (about $112) per month for 20 GB. As with Prolifix, intermediate levels and higher storage quotas are also available.

All these services are constrained by the uplink bandwidth of your Internet connection, and none can make bootable duplicates.

Note: All these services except Tuloy also compress your data, so you may be able to fit much more on their servers than the amounts listed.

On the plus side, Internet backup services keep your files safely off-site with absolutely no effort on your part—and they do so for every backup, not merely on a weekly (or "whenever-I-remember") basis. BackJack, Prolifix, and Datatrieve also encrypt your files (unlike Apple Backup) and make their own redundant, off-site copies of your data (though BackJack charges extra for redundant backups). If, despite my repeated encouragements, you are unable or unwilling to store a set of backup media outside your home or office, an Internet backup service can make that process painless. Even if you do maintain diligent off-site backups, an Internet backup service can provide extra insurance for particularly important files.

These services are no substitute for duplicates. As for archives, unless you have an unusually small home folder, you'll probably find the cost of archiving *all* your personal files over the Internet prohibitive. But, if you can afford it, an Internet backup service may make a reasonable supplement to conventional duplicates and archives, especially for files you're actively working on. Although these services excel in security and ease of use, you must carefully choose which files to include (or exclude) to avoid incurring extremely large bills.

Camcorders

Say you can't afford to buy two or three hard drives. On the other hand, you find optical media too limited in capacity. Then you hear about an amazing product called DV Backup (www.coolatoola.com). This software enables you to use your FireWire-enabled digital camcorder as a backup device. Because MiniDV or Hi8 tapes are relatively inexpensive and easily reusable, media cost is reasonable—but more importantly, you avoid

Amazon S3

Amazon.com recently introduced a service called S3, which provides virtually limitless—yet inexpensive—online storage, complete with encrypted transfer. Could this be the Internet backup solution we've all been waiting for? Maybe in the future, but at the moment, some significant issues exist.

To sign up for Amazon S3, fill out a form (including credit card information) at www.amazon.com/s3/. After your account is activated, Amazon.com provides you with two access keys, both of which you'll need to reach your space on their servers. You can store as much data as you want for $0.15 per gigabyte per month, plus $0.20 per gigabyte transferred (upload or download)—a tiny fraction of what you'd pay for a service like BackJack.

You should be aware of a couple of catches, though. First, you need an application that knows how to communicate with the S3 service, because ordinary FTP, Web, and backup clients cannot. As I write this, the only mainstream Mac Internet client with built-in S3 support is Interarchy (www.interarchy.com; $39). However, a new, free tool called JungleDisk (www.jungledisk.com) performs some magic to mount your S3 storage space as a network volume. JungleDisk handles the back-end communication with S3 and runs a WebDAV server in the background on your local machine; you then connect to that WebDAV server using the Finder's Go > Connect to Server command to access your files.

Because most backup programs can copy files to any mounted volume, they should also be able to work with Amazon S3 via Jungle-Disk, right? Well, maybe. A second catch is that no single file on S3 can be larger than 5 GB. This spells trouble for most archiving schemes (which often produce files or disk images larger than 5 GB). And without using archiving software, you're likely to lose important metadata when copying files. In addition, I've found early versions of JungleDisk to be somewhat finicky; I ran into difficulties getting the virtual network volume to mount and unmount at the right times.

For now, these and other problems limit S3's usefulness for backups. But when full-featured backup programs gain direct support for S3, I expect it'll turn into a fantastic and cost-effective backup option.

the expense of conventional tape drives by pressing into service a device you already own. Best of all, a single 60-minute tape can store as much as 16.5 GB of data, and larger backups can span multiple tapes. You may think this is the ideal solution—what's not to like?

I have rather mixed feelings about using a camcorder as a backup device. Well, not truly mixed: I wouldn't do it myself. All right, if I were stuck on a desert island with just my PowerBook and a camcorder, then maybe; as I mentioned earlier, I believe that something is better than nothing. But for regular, day-to-day use, I worry that your camcorder may actually be worse than nothing.

With all due respect to author Tim Hewett, who has done what can only be called an extraordinary engineering job, DV Backup is at the mercy of your camcorder and tapes, which were not engineered to provide the bit-perfect quality you need for backups. DV Backup, to its credit, does provide user-adjustable error correction as well as an optional data verification pass after recording your data. However, you trade security for speed and capacity; at the highest level of error correction, which essentially puts two copies of each data block on the tape, backups take twice as long as without (logically enough) and use up twice the tape. Because magnetic tape is notoriously error-prone, I wouldn't recommend using anything less than the highest level of protection. But doing so significantly reduces the advantages of this approach.

Here are some other reasons I urge you to think twice before trusting your backups to your camcorder:

- The speed of backups and restoration is much slower even than that of optical media, and nowhere near the speed of hard drives.

- Restoring arbitrary individual files is possible (though time-consuming) only if you store your data uncompressed.

- Your computer monopolizes your camcorder. If you want to shoot video, you have to go without backups for a while (and vice-versa).

- Because digital camcorders were not designed for data backup, the (often miniature) electronics may wear out prematurely due to the frequent stops and starts imposed by backup software.

If you still think a camcorder backup is right for you, you can minimize your risks by observing the following advice:

- Buy high-quality tapes, and use only brand-new tapes for backups. And always stick with the same brand of tape for best results.

- Use the SP speed rather than the LP speed.

- Always use the highest level of error correction; always select the auto-verify option; never use compression.

- Perform test restorations of your data on a regular basis.

- Consider supplementing your camcorder with a secondary backup method, such as periodic backups to optical media.

Joe's Hardware Recommendations

I strongly believe that decisions about hardware should not be made on price alone. You may find the cost per gigabyte of storage to be only $0.15 for DVD-R, for example, versus $1.00 for a hard drive—but that's only part of the story. Speed, convenience, flexibility, and the ability to make bootable backups all add tremendous value to hard drives. Even if you can afford only one external hard drive, making it part of your backup system will pay for itself many times over in saved time and aggravation. If your budget permits, two or even three moderately large external hard drives are definitely the way to go.

That said, if you're looking purely for the most economical hardware path, use your built-in SuperDrive and record backups onto DVD-RW media. Your hardware cost is zero, and $50 should buy you enough blank media to last years.

The Iomega REV comes much closer to the sweet spot at the intersection of capacity, speed, and affordability than optical, magneto-optical, or digital tape media, not to mention Zip and Jaz drives. Assuming REV turns out to be reasonably reliable, it's not a bad choice, but I recommend it only if you can comfortably fit a complete duplicate of your main startup volume within the 35 GB limit of a single REV disk.

11

Choose Your Backup Software

When is a backup program not a backup program? A lot of software that calls itself "backup software" does not actually perform backups in the sense we're discussing here. That is to say, some backup programs do not create additive incremental archives, some do not create duplicates, and some do neither!

Unfortunately, because software developers use terms such as "incremental," "archive," and "backup" differently, you may think you're getting certain capabilities when you buy a product that later turn out to be missing. Thus it is extremely important that you read the fine print, and understand exactly what it is you're looking for.

Duplication Features

Many different applications have the ability to create a bootable backup. This entails copying all the files (including hidden files) on your hard disk to another volume while preserving Unix ownership, permissions, and symbolic links. Assuming you use the correct settings, such applications can also update a duplicate incrementally (rather than recopy every single file each time).

However, you should consider a few other things when looking at a duplication program:

♦ Can it create a bootable duplicate directly onto a hard disk (as opposed to an intermediate disk image or optical media)? If you have an extra hard drive available, you'll want this capability.

♦ Conversely, can it create a restorable duplicate onto optical media or a disk image? Sometimes this feature is useful, other times not.

♦ Can it automatically update the duplicates on a schedule?

♦ When updating a duplicate incrementally, can it also delete files that were deleted on the source volume? If not, your duplicate may include

Retrospect Desktop vs. Retrospect Express

EMC Insignia's Retrospect software comes in several different editions, including Retrospect Desktop ($129) and Retrospect Express (bundled free with some external hard drives and optical drives; also available in a special software bundle from Allume— see Appendix C). The two applications are quite similar, the main differences being that Retrospect Express does not support tape drives or client-server backups and that its facility for selecting or excluding files is more primitive. You can find a list of differences, as well as the features of Retrospect's Workgroup and Server editions, at www.emcinsignia.com/ en/products/mac_compare.dtml. One important issue not on that list: technical support. No matter which version you have, free support is limited to the FAQs, knowledgebase, and community forums on the EMC Web site.

Paid support is available for both products, however; EMC charges $40 per incident for Retrospect Express and $70 per incident for Retrospect Desktop.

In this book, when I refer to "Retrospect" (without any other qualifiers), I mean that the features in question apply to all editions of the program. If a feature is applicable only to a particular edition, I specify "Retrospect Desktop" or "Retrospect Express."

extraneous files that you don't want. (Of the software discussed here that offers both duplication and archiving features, only Personal Backup X lacks the ability to synchronize deletions when updating duplicates.)

♦ Does it have any other features you might use, such as file and folder synchronization?

The duplication programs I've tried are more alike than different, so if you're looking for an application to accomplish this one task, just about anything should do the trick. *Joe's Software Recommendations*, page 151, offers further advice.

Archiving Features

Among applications that provide archiving features, there's a huge range of variation in how they work—and how easy they make it to restore your work later. The fact that an application stores multiple revisions of each backed-up file does not, by itself, make it good for creating archives.

Archive Varieties

First, there's an important distinction to make: true archives versus rotating backups. In a true archive—that is, an additive incremental archive—every version of every file you designate is saved, but identical files are never duplicated. In a *rotating backup*, the program creates a complete, separate copy of all your files every day—basically a non-incremental archive. Then, after a certain number of days (specified by the user), the program erases the oldest backup and adds a new one. Rotating backups, because they copy every single file each day, take longer to perform and require more storage space. If you've got room and time, there's nothing wrong with that approach, and it removes the need for a snapshot list (since all the files are there). However, because you're erasing files older than a certain date, you're restricting your restoration ability. If you keep, say, 5 days worth of rotating backups and find you need a file you deleted a week ago, you're out of luck.

A few applications offer the best of both worlds: *rotating archives*. Like a conventional archive, new files are added to the backup incrementally (without overwriting older versions). However, to conserve space, you can opt to erase the oldest versions of selected files at the same time—for example, all versions older than 30 days, or versions copied more than 30 sessions ago.

Warning! Not every program uses the same criteria to determine when a file should be added to an incremental archive. Some rely exclusively on modification dates, which is an error-prone method. For instance, simply changing the name of a file does not change its modification date. And some applications do not correctly set the modification date each time you save a file.

♦   *Most backup software is intelligent enough to figure out when a file has changed, regardless of its modification date—or at least provide an option to check other criteria. But some is not. Worse, unless you carefully crosscheck archived files against the originals, you may not notice such an error until it's too late.*

♦   *The best way to guard against this problem (apart from buying high-quality backup software) is to spot-check the modification dates of files from applications you use frequently to be sure they were correctly updated the last time you saved them.*

♦   *If you encounter files that do not reflect the correct modification dates, try downloading the free (donations accepted) contextual menu plug-in TouchCM. After installing the plug-in, select the files in question, Control-click (or right-click), and choose Touch from the contextual menu to set the modification date to the current time and date (www.exittoshell.com/products/touch.shtml).*

File Format, Compression, and Encryption

To oversimplify somewhat, most software employs one of two basic methods to copy files when performing a backup. One way is to copy each file in a stand-alone Finder-readable format, so that the backed-up files look exactly like the originals. Another way is to copy all the files into a single, larger file (sometimes called an archive file or a backup set). Each approach has advantages and disadvantages.

Finder-format copies can be restored without the use of a backup program—just drag and drop. Some people also feel more secure knowing they can get at their files easily even if their backup software goes south. Of course, the backed-up files generally take up exactly as much space as the originals (see just ahead for a discussion of RsyncX, which changes this equation somewhat).

Archive files can be compressed as they're stored, potentially saving a large amount of hard disk space. They can also be encrypted, so that if your backup media were lost or stolen, no one could read your files without knowing your passphrase. And unlike Finder copies, which normally take as their owner the user name of the person currently logged in, archive files can preserve original Unix ownership and permissions. Of course, you will need the backup software to restore files, and you could have a slightly higher risk of data loss due to file corruption (since all the data is stored in a single file)—but most backup software has verification mechanisms to compensate for this.

Note: Not all programs that offer compression or encryption copy data into a single archive file. A few can compress or encrypt individual files, such that they can be moved or copied (but not opened) in the Finder. You must still use the backup software to restore them to their original state.

RsyncX (based on the open-source command-line program rsync) deserves special mention here. Its unique copying method produces space-saving incremental archives that nevertheless look and act like complete Finder-readable copies. Here's how it works: When you perform your first archive backup, RsyncX makes a complete copy of the selected files—with Unix ownership and permissions intact. When the next incremental backup runs, the program creates a new folder that *appears* to contain another complete copy of all your files. In reality, only modified files are copied; for files that have not changed, RsyncX uses a Unix trick to create a link to the original copy that appears in the Finder to be an ordinary file. This link functions somewhat like an alias in that it takes up virtually no space and merely points to another file. But when you copy this special link to another volume (when restoring files, say), you automatically copy the entire file. The upshot of this technique is that RsyncX comes quite close to offering the best of both worlds: Finder-readable files that require no more space than an archive file.

However, you should also be aware of another option: disk images. Some backup software, at least when backing up to a hard disk, stores files in a disk image. (Apple Backup 3 uses this technique, although its disk images are hidden inside packages that look like ordinary files.) Like an archive file, a disk image is a single file that contains all your other files—and can optionally be compressed, encrypted, or both. The difference is that you can double-click a disk image, and after supplying the passphrase (if necessary) it will mount on the Desktop as a regular volume—after which you can read and copy files using the Finder. Sounds great, doesn't it? It can be, but keep in mind that in most cases, each incremental archive backup is stored on a *separate* disk image, so without a snapshot or file list provided by the backup software (see *Snapshots and File Lists,* just ahead), restoration can be quite involved.

When making a duplicate onto another hard disk, Finder copies are obviously mandatory. For archives, though, I strongly prefer a format that offers both compression and encryption—and in this respect, archive files are generally more elegant and convenient than disk images.

Note: Maxtor OneTouch drives include software with a feature called DiskLock, which prevents access to the drive's contents unless you enter a password. DiskLock does not encrypt the drive's contents, though—it merely hides them. This feature may protect your data from a casual snoop, but it won't stop a determined hacker nearly as effectively as encryption will.

Snapshots and File Lists

When it comes time to restore files from an archive, you must be able to locate the versions you're looking for quickly and easily. Some backup programs facilitate such restorations by offering *snapshots*—lists of all the files on your computer as they existed at the time of each backup, even if they were already present in the archive and therefore not copied during that particular session. Suppose you want to restore all the files on your machine as they existed last Tuesday. Having a list of all the files as they appeared on Tuesday—and an automated way to restore them—can be extremely valuable.

On the other hand, imagine that you want to look back at every version of just one particular file as it existed over the past month. In this case, you don't want to wade through snapshots—you simply want a list (sorted by file name or date—or better yet, searchable) of each version of the file in the archive, from which you can choose just the ones you want. Without either a snapshot or a file list, you'll need to locate each version of the file manually—often in a series of dated folders. This makes for a long and tedious restoration process.

Sources and Destinations

The volume *from* which you back up files is known as the *source;* the volume *to* which you back them up is known as the *destination* (or *target*). Be sure the software you select can accommodate the sources and destinations you wish to use.

All backup programs can copy data from your startup disk. Most can also copy data from other attached hard drives, network volumes (including AppleShare volumes, FTP servers, and iDisks mounted in the Finder). And usually you can select arbitrary folders or files anywhere on those volumes to be backed up. However, there are exceptions. Backup Simplicity, for example, supports only your startup volume.

Note: Even if your backup software supports copying files from a mounted network server, you will generally be unable to make a *bootable* backup of a network volume.

In most cases, your range of destination options also includes any Finder-mountable volume. (So, theoretically you could even back up one network volume to a different network volume if you wanted to.) If you wish, you can even back up your files onto a disk image. Most programs require that you manually create the disk image yourself using Disk Utility and mount it in the Finder before you can use it as a backup destination.

A similar issue comes into play with optical media. A backup program can support recordable CDs and DVDs as a destination in either of two senses:

♦ You pop a blank disc into your drive, give it a name, and allow it to mount in the Finder. The backup software sees the disc as a possible destination like any other volume. After running the backup program, you then return to the Finder to manually burn and eject the disc.

♦ The backup program itself asks for blank media when needed, writing to it directly without the intervention of the Finder.

The first way of supporting optical media is trivially easy for software developers to implement, so that is how many backup programs work. But this approach does have some problems. First, it requires much more human intervention—performing manual steps despite the fact that the backup itself runs automatically on a schedule. Second, it eliminates the possibility of *multisession* recording (the ability to record additional chunks of information on a partially used disc after the initial write session) since the Finder does not include this feature. This is a problem because without multisession capability, you will use a much larger number of discs—increasing not only media cost, but inconvenience. (Note, however, that some applications, including Retrospect, use a packet-writing technique to add data to partially used optical discs. This is even more efficient than multisession support, but it means that only the application used to record the discs can read them later.) Therefore, if you need to record backups onto optical media, I strongly recommend using an application with multisession (or packet-writing) support.

A related issue is what I'm going to call *media spanning*. Suppose you have more data than will fit on a single CD or DVD—or even that you have a single file that's too large to fit on a single disc. Some backup programs intelligently manage backups that span multiple discs, prompting you for new media when required during a backup (splitting files if necessary), and asking for the proper discs when restoring files (rejoining split files). Although the need for media spanning could affect those backing up onto hard drives as well, it's most crucial for those using optical media. Only a few backup programs offer media spanning, and even fewer include both media spanning and multisession or packet-writing support.

Selectors and Exclusions

Selective archive backups do not include every file on your hard disk. But archiving even your entire home folder may be overkill, since it includes things like cache files, which serve no useful purpose in the context of a backup, and digital media files (such as MP3s ripped from your CD collection), which, because they change infrequently, are adequately backed up by your duplicates. So instead of selecting one or more folders to archive, you may wish to explicitly include or exclude certain types of files.

Some backup programs include user-definable criteria specifying which files should be included (selectors) or excluded (exclusions) from a particular folder or volume—and a few programs offer both. Depending on the program, these criteria may include file names, sizes, Finder labels, extensions, modification dates, and any number of other factors.

In general, I find exclusions more useful than selectors, though I would not generally consider either an absolute must in a backup program. Your mileage, of course, may vary.

Ease of Restoration

No matter how easy it is to back up your hard disk, if your software makes it difficult to restore files, you're going to be unhappy with it. After all, a backup that you can't restore is worthless. Backup programs typically offer one of three main approaches to restoration:

♦ **Finder restoration:** The backup program has no Restore command; to restore files, you drag them manually from the backup volume onto your hard disk. This is fine if you're restoring an entire folder, but if you've done an additive incremental archive, you may have to sort through dozens or hundreds of folders to locate the right versions of each of your files.

♦ **Reverse backup:** In this scheme, the backup program once again does not offer a Restore command, instead it expects that you'll swap the source and destination locations and perform your backup again—in reverse. While this may reduce manual effort somewhat, it's still going to be a hassle when restoring versioned files from an archive (except, perhaps, in the case of RsyncX, as I discussed previously). And even in the best cases, a reverse backup can be confusing and stressful, because it's easy to get the source and destination mixed up when their contents are so similar.

♦ **A Restore command:** The backup program (usually) keeps track of all the files you backed up during each session, allowing you to copy them back to their proper locations—or another destination of your choice—with a few clicks. In most cases, before starting the restoration, you can choose a subset of the files, or even pick out one version of a single file if that's all you need. Restore commands and snapshots tend to appear together.

It probably goes without saying that I prefer applications with a Restore command—they make the restoration quicker and easier. Of course, the presence of a Restore feature does not, by itself, mean the process will be easy, but it's a hopeful sign.

Restoring a Full Archive as a Bootable Volume

If you choose to perform a full (rather than selective) archive, bear in mind that not all backup software can restore your archive from an arbitrary point to a blank disk in such a way that the resulting volume will be bootable. In order for a restored full archive to be bootable, several things must be true:

♦ All files needed for your Mac to start up—including a great many hidden files—must be included in the backup and restored afterward.

♦ The backup software must preserve Unix ownership, permissions, and symbolic links during the backup process and the restoration process; doing so requires that you enter an administrator's password.

♦ When restoring the files, the destination disk must not contain any extraneous files that could interfere with booting; normally, this implies erasing the disk before restoring the archive.

Most backup software that provides both duplication and archiving features also enables you to restore a full archive as a bootable volume, assuming that you set it up properly. Some programs, however (notably Synchronize Pro X), can restore a bootable volume only from a duplicate, not from an archive. A few applications permit full archives to be restored as bootable volumes, but lack a snapshot feature—meaning you must manually locate and copy a large number of documents to return your disk to the state you wish to recreate.

Unfortunately, most backup software does not explicitly state whether or not it can restore a full archive as a bootable volume, and of the programs that do, some are more reliable in this regard than others. This may be a good reason to consider performing selective backups instead; on the other hand, if full archives are important to you, I recommend using Retrospect.

Ease of Use

In addition to ease of restoration, an application's overall ease of use is also important. The interface should be self-explanatory—ideally, clear enough that you can figure out how to perform a basic backup and restoration without ever looking at a manual.

If your backup software is difficult to learn or set up, you're less likely to use it. So you want an application you can configure in an hour or so—not something that takes you an entire day to figure out. You also want your backup software to perform its duties on a schedule with as little interruption to your routine as possible. The best backup software would be completely invisible, working silently behind the scenes until you needed it.

Even so, don't underestimate the importance of good documentation. A well-written manual can be a godsend when trying to comprehend the minutiae of rotating archives or client-server configuration.

Support and Reputation

Some backup software is published by individuals who like to program in their spare time. At the other end of the spectrum, some backup software is published by large corporations with a small army of programmers and a full-time, paid technical support staff. Ironically, I've often received better and quicker technical support from individual authors—even those who give away their applications for free—than big companies. On the other hand, if you're entrusting all the data on the computers in your home or small office to a backup application, you may feel more comfortable knowing that a professional staff stands behind the product.

Rolling Your Own with Unix Utilities

Since backups are essentially a matter of copying files, many industrious Mac users have chosen to wrap up a few Unix commands in a shell script (with or without a nice Aqua interface) and call it a backup program. Under Tiger, Apple's included command-line tools (such as cp and tar) have the capability of copying files with both data forks and resource forks intact; under Panther, Apple's ditto tool serves this purpose (see the Glossary for info on data and resource forks). Third-party tools, such as rsync, can do the same, and with proper use, these tools can also maintain the correct creator, type, owner, and permissions settings. Certainly a

clever programmer can add a bit of logic to a shell script, employ cron or even iCal to schedule unattended operation, and perhaps use AppleScript Studio to provide a friendly user interface. Indeed, several of the utilities listed in Appendix B were created using this technique.

If you're handy with Unix and want to attempt such an undertaking yourself strictly for fun or as a programming exercise, more power to you. But if your motivation is to save money, I urge you to reconsider. The complex issues one must address in designing backup and restoration routines—particularly for proper additive incremental archives—

will take many hours to work out in even a rudimentary way. Even if you think your time is worth only a few dollars an hour, you'll save yourself both money and grief by purchasing a ready-made backup application.

For one example of a way to use rsync for backups, see Richard Hough's article "Automated Backups on Tiger Using rsync" at O'Reilly's MacDevCenter.com (www.macdevcenter.com/pub/a/mac/2005/07/22/backup.html).

But remember that such a strategy is less sophisticated than what most backup applications can offer—and it comes without any technical support!

Of special note in this regard is EMC Insignia, developers of Retrospect. They charge $70 to speak to a technical support representative on the phone—a seemingly outrageous fee. However, I've used technical support from Dantz (which was purchased by EMC) more than once, and I believe you get what you pay for. The technicians answer promptly, are highly trained, and continue working with you—even over multiple phone calls—until the problem is solved (without charging you for each call). When I'm terrified that I might have just lost all my data and my software doesn't seem to be functioning correctly, I'm only too happy to pay $70 for the reassuring voice and advice of an expert who can help me get things working again.

Price

The backup software included in Appendix B ranges in price from free to $129 (before discounts). The price does not necessarily correlate to capabilities, but I urge you not to skimp when it comes to backup software just to save a few dollars. After all, time is money. If you lose a day of income because your backup program makes you jump through too many hoops when restoring files, that's likely to be a bigger financial hit than the cost of better software.

Joe's Software Recommendations

Having reviewed the most important criteria for selecting backup software, I'd like to give you some specific recommendations. All things being equal, I recommend using a single program for both duplicates and archives. This strategy typically saves you both money and effort, ensures that you will not experience conflicts in schedules or requests for blank media, and generally makes for a less complicated backup system. (However, if you would like to use separate applications for duplicates and archives, see *Duplication Software* and *Archiving Software,* ahead.)

Combination (Duplication+Archiving) Software

The following applications offer both duplication and archiving features as I described them here, as well as scheduled backups:

◆ Backup Simplicity

◆ Data Backup

◆ Déjà Vu

◆ Personal Backup X

◆ Retrospect Desktop

◆ Retrospect Express

◆ RsyncX

◆ Synchronize Pro X

◆ Synk Pro

◆ Tri-Backup

In a pinch, any one of these could potentially do the trick. That's not to say they're equivalent, though—or even adequate for most user's requirements. You can examine each program's features and price in Appendix B to see which one best meets your needs. But allow me to offer some advice:

◆ If you back up to CDs or DVDs, you want software that can automatically split large files to span media and does multisession or packet recording—making Retrospect the only good option.

◆ If you back up to a hard disk, I strongly recommend both compression and encryption; and you shouldn't be forced to create and manage your own disk images to get them. This consideration leaves Data Backup, Retrospect, Synk Pro, and Tri-Backup as candidates.

◆ If ease of restoration is a significant concern to you—and it should be—choose an application that offers snapshots, enabling you to restore all the files from a given point in time in one fell swoop. Your choices once again include Data Backup, Retrospect, and Tri-Backup.

RsyncX also qualifies here; even though it doesn't offer snapshots as I define them, it doesn't truly need them, because each incremental archive effectively functions as its own snapshot. RsyncX's method for storing archives makes restoration from an arbitrary point in time fairly easy.

♦ And finally, if you need to back up multiple computers to a single server, you'll be best served by an application that offers true client-server operation—meaning Retrospect Desktop or RsyncX.

Astute readers may have noticed that Retrospect popped up in each of those lists. Retrospect Desktop is the most expensive of the programs I cover here, at $129 (though you can frequently find it at a significant discount), but it's far and away the most full-featured Mac backup application. It's what most of the authors of the Take Control ebooks use.

Is Retrospect perfect? Certainly not. Some people feel it has a steep learning curve, making it intimidating for less technically inclined users. (I offer advice in Appendix C to help ease your initial configuration.) I've also encountered bugs from time to time—and technical support, should you need it, is pricey. In addition, EMC Insignia is sometimes slow to add support for newer storage devices; if you buy the latest and greatest optical drive, you may have to wait several months before a Retrospect update includes the necessary driver. (FireWire hard drives are always supported automatically.)

Even so, if I had to recommend just one application from this group, it would be Retrospect Desktop. (If you happen to purchase a drive that includes a free copy of Retrospect Express, that's an equally good option unless you need to perform client-server network backups.) If $129 is too pricey, Data Backup would be my second choice, edging out Tri-Backup slightly in ease of use and reputation of the developer.

Duplication Software

The following applications (including some that bill themselves as "backup" or "synchronization" software) can create bootable backups but *not* additive incremental archives:

- BounceBack Professional

- Carbon Copy Cloner[1]

- Clone'X

- CopyCatX

- FoldersSynchronizer

- MimMac

- SilverKeeper

- QuickBack (part of SpeedTools Utilities)

- SuperDuper!

- Xupport

Although each of these applications has a different interface and a variety of additional features, as far as I'm concerned they're all more or less equally capable in terms of making a bootable backup of an entire hard disk. Most of these applications offer limited-time demos or trial versions, so if you're considering such an application, you can download a copy and make sure it meets your needs before making a purchase.

If I had to recommend just one program from this list, however, I'd give the nod to SuperDuper!—in addition to a thorough feature set, it excels at giving plain-English explanations of what it's about to do, making a potentially troubling task much less nerve-wracking. It also preserves some metadata that some other utilities don't, making for the most exact copies you can get. Although the full version costs $28, you can use the free demo version to create one-off duplicates; buying a license unlocks features such as scheduling and incremental updates.

But if you happen to have another of these utilities (or prefer a different interface for some reason), any of them should do the job.

---

[1] In order for Carbon Copy Cloner to update your duplicates incrementally, you must also install a program called psync. To do so, click the Preferences button in Carbon Copy Cloner and then click Install Psync. After doing so, select the checkboxes for Synchronize Source to Target and Delete Items Not on Source.

Note: Disk Utility and Duplication. Apple's Disk Utility, included with Mac OS X, can make bootable duplicates. However, I omitted it from the list here and in Appendix B because this feature is obscure (it's a side-effect of a Restore feature) and limited (you have almost zero control over what happens during duplication—and no scheduling capability).

If you *must* use Disk Utility to make a duplicate, you can do so by following these steps:

1. In Disk Utility, select any volume in the list on the left and click the Restore tab.

2. Drag the volume you want to duplicate from the list on the left into the Source field.

3. Drag the destination volume from the list on the left into the Destination field. (This works even though the field looks disabled.)

4. Select the Erase Destination checkbox.

5. Click Restore.

Archiving Software

The following applications offer additive incremental archives, but lack the capability to create bootable backups:

♦ Apple Backup 3 (but not earlier versions)

♦ Archive Assistant (part of StuffIt Deluxe 10.0)

♦ BackupSW

♦ BRU LE

♦ ChronoSync

♦ Dobry Backuper

♦ NTI Shadow

♦ SwitchBack

♦ SyncupX

Unlike the programs that offer only duplication features, these applications vary significantly in their capabilities (see **Table 4** in Appendix B).

As with the combination applications, desirable features for optical media backups include media spanning (offered by Apple Backup, Archive Assistant, BRU LE, and Dobry Backuper) and multisession recording (absent in all of these). Several of these applications, including Apple Backup and Dobry Backuper, require considerable scratch space (up to the size of one disc—CD or DVD), which reduces their usefulness for backing up almost-full volumes.

Compression is found in Apple Backup, Archive Assistant, BRU LE, BackupSW, Datum, and Dobry Backuper, but of these, only Archive Assistant offers encryption. Only BackupSW provides client-server operation (of a sort), and only Apple Backup provides snapshots.

Backup 3: A Big Step Forward

I made no secret of my dislike for Apple's Backup application when it was first released. Backup versions 1 and 2 did not even qualify as backup software in my estimation, since they offered neither archiving nor duplicating capabilities.

But in late September 2005, Apple released an entirely new, rewritten-from-scratch Backup version 3. I'm delighted to be able to say it's no longer terrible! In fact, it has some downright useful features and a comprehensible user interface. Most importantly, it now creates additive incremental archives, thus qualifying it as a "real" backup application.

However (and you knew there would be a "however"), despite these significant improvements, I have a few reservations about Backup 3.

First, it still can't create duplicates. This is not a deal-breaker—you can use any of dozens of other applications to do that, and some of them are even free—but you'll have to set up and maintain two different backup applications.

Second, it only backs up files belonging to the currently logged-in user. If you're the only person using a machine, that's no big deal. But if two or more users share a Mac, each one must log in and run Backup separately to back up that user's files. Virtually all other backup programs can handle data for multiple users at once, correctly maintaining ownership and permissions for each user.

Finally, although Backup 3 can handle optical media just fine (and ably spans your data across multiple discs when necessary),

it cannot write to a given disc in more than one session. So if, during a certain backup run, Backup needed a new DVD for just the last megabyte of data, all the rest of the empty space on that DVD would go to waste. You could not write anything more to it during your next backup run; you'd have to provide a new, blank disc. This limitation can greatly increase your media costs.

I'm happy to recommend Backup as an archiving tool to .Mac members who have just one user account, and who are backing up to hard disks (avoiding the optical media problem just mentioned). For everyone else, though, stick with one of the more mature third-party products such as Retrospect, Data Backup, or Tri-Backup.

BRU LE is a fairly robust application, but it's designed primarily for use with tape libraries. Performing backups to a hard disk or optical media with BRU LE is less than ideal.

NTI Shadow has a unique capability: the option to archive a copy of selected files *every time you save them*. In this way, it functions as a cross between a backup utility and a version-control application.

With the exception of Apple Backup, which has a snapshot capability, all the applications in this list make the restoration of an arbitrary day's worth of files unnecessarily complicated. Unlike earlier versions, Apple Backup 3 now offers very respectable capabilities and a reasonable interface. *If* you're a .Mac member, and *if* you're backing up to hard drives, and *if* you're the only user on your machine, Backup 3 makes a fine choice, and you can get it without any additional expense. (See the sidebar on the opposite page for more information.) However, if you don't meet those criteria, you can get a better solution for less money.

In other words: most people are better off sticking with one of the applications discussed earlier that can handle both duplicates and archives—in particular, Retrospect, Data Backup, or Tri-Backup.

Set Up Your Backup System

You've laid out a backup strategy, procured the necessary hardware and software, and now have a stack of boxes, cables, and discs on your desk. Now what? Time to set everything up, run your first backups, and verify that they work the way you were expecting. Because I don't know which hardware and software you've selected, I can't give you detailed instructions for installation and setup. However, I want to outline some procedures you should always follow.

Test Hardware First

If you've purchased hard drives or other external devices, connect them and make sure your computer can write to and read from them before installing your backup software. Although I've seen a few cases in which a backup application can communicate with a device that does not otherwise appear visible to the computer, you are unlikely to encounter such a situation with hard drives and optical drives. If you connect a device after installing your backup software and it does not work, it will be harder to determine whether the device or the software is at fault.

Partition Hard Disks

If you're using hard drives for backups, you may wish to partition the disks. (To determine how large each partition should be, review *Does Size Matter?*, page 118.) To partition a hard disk:

1. After connecting the drive, launch Disk Utility.

2. From the list on the left, select the hard disk you want to partition, and click the Partition tab on the right.

3. Under Volume Scheme, choose the number of partitions you want. For each partition, give it a name, and choose a format. Mac OS Extended (Journaled) is the default and recommended choice.

    Warning! *If you want to be able to boot into Mac OS 9 from this volume (and if your machine supports that option), be sure the Install Mac OS 9 Disk Drivers checkbox is selected. (This setting applies to the whole disk, not to a particular volume.) You can't change this later without erasing the disk again, so if in doubt, leave the box checked.*

Partitioning without Reformatting?

Four new utilities promise the capability of partitioning your hard disk *without* having to reformat it first, preserving all your data. I haven't tested them thoroughly, so I strongly recommend that you not attempt to repartition a drive without backing it up first.

Drive Genius: This $99 application from Prosoft Engineering includes disk testing, repair, and optimization features. You can also use it to add, delete, or resize partitions without reformatting a drive—though the current version cannot merge two partitions while keeping the data from both intact (www.prosofteng.com).

VolumeWorks: The $60 VolumeWorks from SubRosaSoft is basically the partitioning portion of Drive Genius packaged as a stand-alone product (www.subrosasoft.com).

DiskStudio: Micromat's DiskStudio is a $50 application that provides only partitioning tools, not testing or repair. Like Drive Genius, it can add partitions without erasing data or delete partitions while leaving the rest of the disk intact. However, it currently offers no mechanism for *resizing* partitions (www.micromat.com).

iPartition: From Coriolis Systems, the $45 iPartition, like DiskStudio, is strictly a partitioning tool. Unlike DiskStudio, it has the capability of resizing partitions without erasing your data. The only significant limitation is that it does not include its own bootable CD—to use it on your startup disk, you must boot from another volume or create your own bootable CD that includes iPartition (www.coriolis-systems.com).

4. Resize the partitions manually by dragging the dividers, or enter a size for each partition.

5. When you're happy with your settings, click Partition. You can then quit Disk Utility.

Your hard disk is now partitioned into multiple volumes, each of which will show up in the Finder as an independent disk.

Install and Test Software

Installing backup software may be a simple matter of dragging a downloaded file to your Applications folder, or you may need to run a more complex installer. In any case, follow the developer's directions to install your backup software now.

Tip: If you have more than one startup volume (not counting duplicates), consider installing your backup software onto each of them. This will make things easier if your main disk is unavailable and you need to restore files.

Read, or at least thoroughly skim, the documentation that came with your backup software. Acquaint yourself with the terminology the program uses and how its features are organized. Backup programs are notorious for being unintuitive, so spending some time with the manual before you do any heavy-duty configuration will save you grief later.

Next, just to get your feet wet, try backing up one arbitrary file (or small folder) from one volume to another—and then restoring it. This seemingly small step can go a long way toward helping you to understand how the software works.

Label Media and Files

Most backup programs ask you to give descriptive names to each recurring backup procedure—"Daily Archive," "Weekly Duplicate," "Backup Set A," or whatnot. Some applications use these names to label archives, bookmarks, catalogs, or other files stored as part of the backup, while others simply use them as an internal reference. In any case, applications usually make a distinction between the name of a given backup and the name of the media on which it is stored. You may duplicate a volume named "Greg" onto a volume named "Marcia," and you may store your daily archive, which you've named "Backup Set Delta," onto a volume named "Cindy." If you aren't careful with these names, confusion can easily result.

I strongly recommend consistency and clarity in names. Here are some specific guidelines:

◆ If using hard disks, give each volume (disk or partition) a different name in the Finder. Although you can use sequential letters or numbers to label the volumes, longer and more meaningful names may be less confusing. For example, if you use two rotating disks, each partitioned into two volumes, the first drive might have a piece of tape on it with the name "Bart." Bart could be partitioned into a volume named "Bart Duplicate Disk" and another named "Bart Archive Disk"; another drive, labeled "Lisa," would have "Lisa Duplicate Disk" and "Lisa Archive Disk." Notice that I used the word "Disk" to differentiate the name of the volume from the name of the backup procedure.

◆ Resist the temptation to name the backup disks the same as the source disks! After all, you'll still be able to boot from "Greg" if duplicated onto "Homer Duplicate Disk."

◆ If your software asks you to label backup procedures, scripts, files, or backup sets, follow a similar pattern, but add the frequency. For example: "Bart Weekly Duplicate" or "Lisa Daily Archive." And be sure to store a given backup on media with the corresponding label! That way you can easily keep track of which backup is stored on which media, without getting the labels of the procedures confused with the labels of the volumes.

- Put *physical* labels on all media (which could be writing on a CD with a marker or sticking a piece of masking tape on a hard drive case). The label should indicate the names of the volume(s) on the media.

- For multi-CD or -DVD sets, be sure to label each disc separately, following the name and sequence number the software gives it.

Set Up Duplicates

With your hardware and software installed, it's time to configure your first serious backup: a duplicate of your startup volume. The exact procedure varies from one application to the next, but I walk you through the basics.

Tip: For detailed instructions on setting up duplicates in Retrospect, see *Set Up a Duplicate Script* (page 196).

In your backup application, select the function for making a bootable backup. Some applications distinguish between commands that are performed immediately and commands that can be performed on a schedule. Given the choice, select the option that can be scheduled.

Some applications require that you select a checkbox or otherwise indicate whether Unix ownership and permissions should be preserved; for duplicates, they should. If the application includes an option to follow aliases and symbolic links, be sure to *deselect* it.

If requested, give your duplication procedure a descriptive name, and select a source and destination volume. Keep in mind that the destination volume, if a hard disk or partition, must be at least as large as the amount of data on the source volume. Also, check to see that the destination volume does not ignore ownership; if it does, your duplicate will not be bootable. To check this, select the destination volume's icon in the Finder and choose File > Get Info. In the Ownership & Permissions portion of the window, make sure the checkbox labeled Ignore Ownership On This Volume is *deselected*.

You may have an option to turn incremental duplication on or off. If so, be sure to turn it on! Otherwise, every time you perform the duplication, the application will copy every single file on your hard disk, even though most of them have not changed.

If your application offers compression and encryption, be sure to turn them off. On the other hand, if it offers *verification* (checking that files were written properly), turn it on. Without verification, errors in writing files may go unnoticed, and even a tiny error in a single file could prevent your duplicate from working properly.

Finally, start the backup. Often this is just a matter of clicking a "Backup" button. (I cover adding a schedule for this script later in *Automate Your Backups,* page 170.)

Now wait. Even if you have a fast computer, a fast hard drive, and a fast interface, duplicates can take some time. In some cases, you'll be able to continue using your computer while the files are being copied, but re-member that if you modify files during this process, the duplicate will no longer be an accurate copy of your entire hard disk as it existed at a single point in time. It may be worth noting how much, if at all, the operation of your computer slows down while a backup is in progress, because this could affect when you schedule backups to run.

After testing your duplicate (next paragraph), you can repeat this proce-dure to set up duplicates on additional hard disks or other media. If you are creating duplicates of more than one volume, set up those additional volumes at the same time.

Test Your Duplicate

Even if your backup application reported no errors, you should test the duplicate to make sure it truly is bootable. If your duplicate was stored directly on another hard disk, testing it is easy. (If it was stored on optical media, see *Restore a CD/DVD Duplicate onto a Hard Disk,* page 178.) Follow these steps:

1. Open System Preferences and click the Startup Disk icon.

2. Select the volume where your duplicate is stored. (You *did* give it a unique name, right?)

Note: If you duplicated your hard disk to an external drive connected to a server, you must physically connect that drive directly to the Mac you want to start up. If it's on another machine, it will not appear in the Startup Disk preference pane. The only way to boot a Mac over a network is to use NetBoot to load a special disk image stored on a central machine running Mac OS X Server; an ordinary hard drive won't work, even if it contains a bootable copy of Mac OS X.

---

3. Click Restart.

4. After your computer restarts, verify that it used your duplicate as the startup volume. If your Finder preferences are set to display mounted hard disks on the Desktop, the one shown at the top is your startup volume. (To set this preference, choose Finder > Preferences, click the General icon, and make sure the Hard Disks checkbox is selected.)

   If your computer did not start from the correct volume, restart it again, holding down the Option key until the screen displays icons for each of the valid startup volumes. Click the volume you wish to use and then click the right arrow button to complete the startup process.

Tip: If your computer refuses to boot from a FireWire drive even after holding down the Option key at restart, one possible cause is a conflict with other FireWire devices (such as an iSight camera). Disconnect all other FireWire devices from your system and try again with only your external hard drive attached.

5. Do a few spot checks to confirm that important files are where they should be, that you have network access (try viewing a Web page), and that a few applications launch. I recommend *not* checking your email, though, as doing so may download messages and delete the originals from the server—you'll miss them when you return to your usual startup disk.

6. Return to System Preferences, click the Startup Disk icon, choose your usual startup disk, and click Restart.

You've just confirmed that your duplicate works correctly. If your computer does not restart from your duplicate volume, however, your backup software may have malfunctioned. Try performing the duplication again, consult your software's documentation, or contact the developer's technical support department for assistance.

Note: Using an External Drive as a Startup Volume. All modern Macs (those manufactured since approximately 2000) can boot from an external FireWire hard drive, assuming the drive was manufactured to the proper specifications; Intel-based Macs can also boot from USB 2.0 drives. See the sidebar *USB 2.0 Drives, Intel Macs, and Bootability* (page 121), for more information.

If you have trouble booting from an external drive, check Apple's Web site to confirm that your machine supports booting from the interface you're using. Also check the drive manufacturer's site to see whether any firmware updates are available for your drive.

Set Up Archives

Next, configure your archive backups. As with duplicates, the exact procedure varies from one application to the next, but again, I give you a basic overview.

Tip: You can find detailed instructions for creating Retrospect archives in *Set Up a Backup Server Script* (page 200).

In your backup application, select the function appropriate for making an archive. (Appendix B has notes on how some applications name this feature.) Note again that some applications distinguish between commands that are performed immediately and commands that can be performed on a schedule. Given the choice, select the option that can be scheduled. If requested, give your archive procedure a descriptive name.

Select your source(s). This may be a simple matter of navigating to your home folder, or it may involve adding many different folders from all over your hard disk. See *Archive Strategy* (page 105) for details on choosing which files to include in an archive. If you wish (and if supported by your software), choose selectors or exclusions.

Select your destination. If you are archiving files to a hard disk, choose that disk. You may wish to create a new folder on that disk to contain your backups, especially if the disk also holds other files.

If you're storing your archive on optical media or a disk image, some backup software requires that you first mount the volume in the Finder. To do this:

♦ For blank optical media, simply insert the disc into your drive; when prompted, give the disc a name and choose the (admittedly confusing) action Open Finder. (This is not required in Retrospect, which can write directly to optical media. When creating your backup set, choose "CD/DVD" as the backup set type.)

♦ For a disk image, launch Disk Utility (located in /Applications/Utilities) and choose Images > New > Blank Image. Specify a name and location for the image. Select Sparse Disk Image as the format, meaning that the image will automatically grow as necessary to accommodate more files, with its *initial* size being whatever you select from the Size pop-up menu. Optionally (but recommended) choose AES-128 from the Encryption pop-up menu. Click Create, and if you previously chose to encrypt the image, specify a passphrase when prompted. Disk Utility automatically mounts the new image in the Finder, ready to be used by your backup software.

Some software requires you to specify whether your backups should be incremental or additive (though the terminology differs with each application; once again, see Appendix B for notes on how some applications name these features). If so, be sure to select those features now.

If your application offers compression and encryption and you have not already turned them on, consider doing so now. Compression will slow your backup but enable it to occupy much less space—normally a good thing. If you select encryption, choose a secure passphrase—and don't

FileVault and Backups

Mac OS X's FileVault feature optionally encrypts the entire contents of your home folder, so that your files are protected from prying eyes and thieves. It accomplishes this behind the scenes by storing your home folder in an encrypted disk image. Using File-Vault may complicate backups.

If you ask your backup software to archive the entire disk image, it will be unable to perform incremental archives of your home folder, instead making a complete copy of the image each time it runs. This is because, from the point of view of the backup soft-

ware, your entire home folder is a single file—so any change to the data in your home folder, no matter how small, must result in that entire FileVault disk image being copied again.

You can work around this problem by instructing your software to ignore the FileVault disk image and instead look only at the files stored within it; you must then make sure your FileVault-protected home folder is unlocked and mounted when your backup software runs. However, if you have backups running when you are not at your machine, an un-

locked FileVault disk image can jeopardize the security of your files. For this reason, if you must use FileVault, you should schedule backups to begin when you are physically present.

But my recommendation, instead, is to avoid using FileVault in the first place. Backup concerns aside, the way FileVault stores your data in day-to-day use makes it extremely vulnerable to corruption; theoretically, even a tiny amount of damage could render your entire home folder unusable.

forget it! Also, if the software offers *verification* (checking to see that files were written properly), turn it on. Verification alerts you to errors in writing files that may otherwise go unnoticed and cause problems when you try to restore the files.

Finally, start the backup. Often this is just a matter of clicking a "Backup" button. (I describe adding a schedule for this script next, in *Automate Your Backups.*)

After testing your archive, you can repeat this procedure to set up archives to additional hard drives or other media.

Test Your Archive

When the backup is complete, test it by choosing a few random files or folders from the archive to restore. If your backup software has a Restore feature, use it; if not, select your former destination volume as the source. To test your archive, follow these steps:

1. **Restore to a different location:** You can usually restore files either to their original locations or to another location of your choice. For this test, restore your selected files to a *different* location—say, your Desktop folder or another spot where you can find them easily.

2. **Check the restored files:** Compare the restored files to the originals using the Finder's File > Get Info command. Each pair of files should match exactly: same name, size, icon, creation date, and modification date. If the files were not copied to your selected destination or they are not identical, then either your backup software or its user made an error! Check your software's documentation, and if necessary contact the developer's technical support department for assistance.

3. **Try an in-place restoration:** Temporarily move one of the original files you backed up to a different location (again, the Desktop folder works well for this), then use your application's Restore feature to restore the file to its original location.

4. **Check the restored files:** Again, check each file carefully to make sure it is correct.

If the files are correct regardless of the location to which you restored them, your archive is working properly.

Tip: Although your initial test of a backup may succeed, it's important to test backups regularly to confirm that the archives are still intact, and that all the required files are being updated as they should be. If you're unaware of an error that has been preventing your backups from running properly for the past few months, the consequences could be severe. Get in the habit of doing a test restoration every time you change your car's oil or test the batteries in your smoke detector. By the way, if you haven't changed your oil or tested the batteries in your smoke detector recently... now might be a good time.

Automate Your Backups

Now that you have successfully performed and tested both a duplicate and an archive, it's time for the last important step: scheduling these backups to occur automatically.

Any backup software worth its salt will make it easy to put a given backup procedure on a simple, recurring schedule—e.g., Daily Archive every night at 11:00 p.m., Weekly Duplicate every Sunday morning at 6:00 a.m. But if you have multiple sets of media, creating an alternating backup schedule can be more complex. In this case, you might want Bart Daily Archive to be stored on Bart Archive Disk every night this week, while Lisa Daily Archive is stored on Lisa Archive Disk every night next week, and so on. Instructions for setting up such schedules in Retrospect are in Appendix C.

When choosing times and days for your backups to run, keep in mind these considerations:

◆ Will the destination media be ready? If not, will you be available to insert or enable it?

◆ Do you need to supply a password—for the backup software itself, or to mount a network volume? If you cannot store such passwords in your Keychain, or do not wish to do so, be sure the backups run when you're present to enter the passwords.

♦ Will the backup slow down your computer? If so, think about scheduling it for a time when you're not busy.

Regardless of your software, begin by scheduling your archives, which will probably run every day. Then schedule duplicates, choosing a time of day well before (or after) your scheduled archive run to avoid conflicts between the two schedules. Repeat as necessary for each media set you will be using.

Be sure to make a note of your duplication schedule in your favorite calendar application or on a paper calendar so that you will know when to swap media for off-site storage. For example, if you do a weekly duplicate

Power Management and Backups

Although this may seem self-evident, a scheduled backup will not run unless your computer is already turned on and awake at the scheduled time. Some people leave their computers running all the time, perhaps setting the display to dim or the hard drive to spin down after a certain amount of idle time to save energy. However, if you normally turn off your computer or put it to sleep when you're done using it—or if you have it set to go to sleep automatically—you may run into problems with scheduled backups. In most cases, these problems are easily solved with a bit of foresight.

Power management on a Mac is controlled using the Energy Saver pane of System Preferences. If you click the Schedule tab, you'll see a checkbox labeled "Start Up the Computer." What it does not tell you is that this setting will also *wake up* a computer at the scheduled time if it's on but asleep. If you select that checkbox and enter the days and times corresponding to your backup schedule (say, Every Day at 2:00 AM), the machine will turn itself on (or wake itself up) at the appropriate times. However, a few words of caution:

♦ Be sure to select times at least 5 minutes before your backups are scheduled, to allow the computer time to start up completely.

♦ If you configured your Mac to request your password when you turn it on or wake it up, the computer may get stuck at the Log In screen when you're not there. To turn off the password prompts, first go to the Security pane of System Preferences and deselect the checkboxes labeled "Require password to wake this computer from sleep or screen saver" and "Disable automatic login." Then go to the Accounts pane and click the Login Options icon near the bottom on the left. Select "Automatically Log In As," choose your user name from the pop-up menu, and enter your password when prompted.

♦ You can also use the Schedule pane of Energy Saver Preferences to turn off your computer (or put it to sleep) after completing a backup. If you do this, be sure to allow plenty of time; full backups sometimes take hours.

on Sunday, you might create a recurring reminder to swap media every Monday morning before work.

After setting your backups on a schedule, check them periodically to make sure they are running as you expect. Some backup software provides logs for this purpose—or you can look at the files on the backup media and confirm that they are as recent as they should be.

Mind Your Media

So you've got your carefully labeled hard drives, DVDs, or other media with freshly recorded data. Now what?

Taking care of your media is just as important as making proper backups in the first place. If the media is lost or damaged, it does you no good. So I want to say a few words about handling, storing, and caring for backup media.

Whether you use hard drives, optical discs, or another type of media, the same general rules apply: store them in a cool, dry place away from significant sources of light, static electricity, vibration, and other hazards (such as inquisitive pets or children). All this may seem obvious, but it pays to remember that you're doing backups in the first place because your data is valuable—perhaps even irreplaceable. So treat your media with care.

Note: For extra safety, store your media in a container that's rated fireproof for media.

Recycling vs. Long-Term Archives

If you use hard drives for backups, sooner or later they will fill up. (Whether this takes a few months or a few years depends on the rate at which you accumulate new data and the size of your backup disks.) And if you use lower-capacity removable media, sooner or later you will have a stack so large it threatens to collapse under its own weight. When this happens, you have two options: buy completely new media and start over, or recycle.

By "recycle" I don't mean throw your backups in a blue bin—I mean erase the media and reuse it for a new set of backups.

One argument for starting fresh is that new media is virtually always more reliable than old media. Another is that you can save your old media as a long-term archive, in case you need to see what was on your computer a few years ago. On the other hand, recycling media saves money, not to mention physical storage space. And most people have little need for backups stretching back more than a couple of years.

The cost of buying a new stack of DVD-R discs is, of course, much lower than the cost of buying new hard drives. In addition, as I mentioned earlier, hard drives make a poor choice for long-term storage (though an older hard drive that you wouldn't trust for backups may be fine for casual, non-critical uses). So, if you use hard disks to store your backups, you should recycle instead of replace. However, remember that hard drives don't last forever—even if they're just sitting on a shelf, your data will deteriorate over time. A reasonable compromise may be to recycle your hard drives once a year or so for 3 or 4 years, and then replace it. If, when it comes time to erase your drives, you still wish to maintain a copy of the old data, use your backup software to duplicate your archives onto a stack of DVDs first.

Recycle Before Full

For archive backups, you may wish to recycle your media on a regular basis, *before* it fills up. By performing periodic full backups—instead of relying indefinitely on incremental additions since a single full backup long ago—you reduce the risk of data loss due to file corruption or misbehaving backup software. How often you recycle your media is up to you, but in general I'd suggest recycling no less often than every 6 months.

Do, however, be aware that when you recycle media, you lose all the archived files stored since you started that particular cycle. If this makes you nervous, you might consider copying the archive to a set of DVDs before erasing it. In addition, if you recycle more than one set of media (for example, two or three hard drives), stagger them—do one, wait a week or two, then do the next one, and so on. That way, if you suddenly discover that you've erased the archive containing an old file you need, you'll still have a chance to recover it easily from another set of backup media.

Tip: If you're erasing a hard disk anyway, this is a good time to reassess partition sizes (see *Does Size Matter?*, page 118). If your hard disk or home folder is significantly larger than before, consider changing the partition sizes to better accommodate your current needs.

Be careful when erasing a hard disk that contains months or years of backups—especially if you chose not to copy its data onto optical media. For safety, erase just one disk at a time, then perform (and test) regular backups for 1 or 2 weeks before erasing the next disk. If you erase all your backups at once, you're inviting trouble.

Off-Site Storage

Raise your right hand, place your left hand on the nearest sacred text (such as *The Macintosh Bible*), and repeat after me:

I hereby solemnly swear that henceforth, I will at all times maintain a recent, complete set of backup media off-site.

Good. Now I'm going to tell you why you just made such a promise and how to keep it.

No matter how diligently you back up, if something happens to your backup media, you're in trouble. Now, it is safer to keep your backups on an external volume than on, say, another partition of your internal hard disk. But as long as the media on which your backup is stored is physically located near your computer, your data is unsafe. Consider for a moment the range of events that could wipe out both your internal hard drive and any backups in the same area at the same time: fire, flood, earthquake, hurricane, tornado, burglary, destruction by rambunctious children or pets, wayward meteorites. These things all seem so unlikely until they happen to you. Insurance may enable you to replace your hardware and software, but not your data. So please take seriously my advice to keep at least one set of backups *off-site*, by which I mean *in a different building*.

The best approach is to rotate multiple sets of backup media, so that you always have one near your computer and another stored safely somewhere else. Periodically (say, once a week), bring the off-site media back, adding it to your normal backup routine so that it can be updated—and take your most recent local backup off-site.

Tip: When it's time to replace a hard drive completely, you may consider giving away or selling your old drive. Before doing so, be sure to *securely* erase it so that its new owner cannot use a file recovery program to retrieve all your data! Merely dragging files to the Trash will not erase the data in such a way that it cannot be recovered. Even the default Erase feature in Disk Utility won't do the trick. Instead, use a tool that can overwrite the entire disk (including free space, not just particular files) multiple times with random ones and zeroes. Clicking the Options button in Disk Utility's Erase pane provides two ways to zero the data. Other examples of products that include this capability are:

- Shredder (www.dekorte.com/Software/OSX/Shredder/; $5)

- Trash X (www.northernsoftworks.com/; $9)

- ShredIt X (www.mireth.com/; $20)

- SafeShred Pro (www.codetek.com/; $25)

- SPX (http://rixstep.com/4/0/spx/; $39)

- TechTool Pro (www.micromat.com/; $100)

Although you can use this process with just two sets of media, having three makes it more convenient. At any given time, you'll have one set (A) in use, your next-most-recent set (B) on site, and your oldest set (C) off-site. When you rotate the media, you bring your oldest set (C) back on site and make it active, taking what has now become the oldest set (B) off-site—and so on. For maximum safety, if you use only two sets, don't bring your off-site backup media back to your home or office until *after* you've taken another set away; those few hours when all your media is in one place could be the time when disaster strikes.

You may be wondering where exactly "off-site" could be in your case. Here are some suggestions:

- Your place of work

- A neighbor's or relative's home

- A storage unit

Don't keep an off-site backup in your car, which is if anything more susceptible to damage or theft than your home. Heat and cold extremes in your car can also hasten data corruption. If you want as much security as possible with a trade-off of less convenience, keep it in a safe deposit box at your local bank.

Warning! *Because hard disk-based duplicates are, by definition, unencrypted, storing them off-site presents a significant security risk: anyone who obtains the drive also has complete access to your data. Here are some ways of reducing that risk:*

- *Store the drive in a safe deposit box.*

- *Keep all your important data on the drive encrypted within a disk image—perhaps using a utility such as PGPDisk.*

- *Instead of storing the duplicate directly onto a hard disk, put it on an encrypted disk image that's stored on the hard disk. This will require extra steps when it comes time for restoring, but it's much more secure.*

- *Keep (encrypted) archives and (unencrypted) duplicates on separate media, and store only the archives off-site.*

Restore Data from a Backup

If you've followed the directions so far, you've already tested the basic process of booting from a duplicate and restoring individual files from an archive. But in the event your data suffers serious damage, you will want to restore your duplicate, archive, or both onto your main hard disk. Read on for tips to help you through this process.

Repair or Erase Your Disk

If your startup disk (or another volume you've backed up) becomes unusable, you should not copy other files onto it while it's still in an unstable state. In case of serious trouble, the first thing you should do is start up your computer from another volume (a duplicate, a Mac OS X installation CD, or a bootable disk-utility CD such as Alsoft's DiskWarrior). Run Disk Utility or another disk-repair tool to fix any errors on your hard disk. If you are unable to fix the problems, or if they recur even after the utilities have done their best, use Disk Utility to erase the disk before attempting to restore your old files. (And by the way, if you're planning to restore *all* your files, it makes sense to erase the disk first, whether it appears to have any errors or not.)

Restore a Duplicate

If you've booted from your duplicate disk and erased your primary disk, restoring the duplicate onto the primary disk is a piece of cake. (If your duplicate is stored on optical media, see *Restore a CD/DVD Duplicate onto a Hard Disk*, next) Follow the same steps you normally would to create a duplicate, but choose your external disk as the source and your internal disk as the destination. When the duplicate is complete, use the Startup Disk pane of System Preferences to set your internal disk as the startup volume, and restart the computer. If all goes well, your Mac will boot properly from the freshly restored duplicate on your primary disk. Just be careful you don't confuse the backup with the original, especially if they have the same name.

After restoring your duplicate—assuming your last archive update was more recent than your last duplicate update—you'll need to restore your latest set of archived files as well, which I describe in *Restore Archived Files* (page 179).

Restore a CD/DVD Duplicate onto a Hard Disk

Let's say you have a duplicate of your hard disk, stored on a stack of CDs or DVDs. Now it's time to restore them onto your hard disk so you can boot from your duplicate, but your internal hard drive is the only one you have. So there's a problem: If you boot from the internal hard drive (assuming it even has a functioning system), you won't be able to restore the duplicate because that would overwrite files that are actively in use. On the other hand, if you have only one optical drive, you can't boot from that either, because you would then be unable to remove the boot CD/DVD to feed in the backup discs. What to do? The process is tedious, but it can be done. Follow these steps:

1. Start up your computer from your Mac OS X installation CD or DVD—the one that came with your Mac or one you purchased separately.

2. When the first installer screen appears, choose Installer > Open Disk Utility.

3. When Disk Utility opens, select your hard disk, click the Partition tab, and set up at least two partitions on the disk. (If your disk is already partitioned, you can skip this step.) Your goal is to have one partition that's large enough to hold the restored system and another that's large enough to hold a basic installation of Mac OS X. For the latter, a 5 GB partition should be adequate. (Caution: Partitioning your hard disk erases all the data on it.)

4. Quit Disk Utility, return to the installer, and install Mac OS X onto the newly created (small) partition. When asked to choose an installation type (the default is Easy Install), click Customize. Deselect everything except BSD Subsystem. Now proceed with the installation.

5. When the installation is complete, restart your computer from the copy of Mac OS X you've just installed on your small partition.

6. Reinstall your backup software onto the small partition that is currently functioning as your startup volume.

7. Use your software's duplication or restore feature to copy your duplicate from your CDs or DVDs onto the larger partition of your hard disk.

8. Use the Startup Disk pane of System Preferences to select your freshly restored volume as the startup disk, and restart your computer.

You've now restored your duplicate from optical discs to your hard disk.

Restore Archived Files

If you restored files from a duplicate (rather than from a full archive), once your primary hard disk is fully functional, your last step is to update it with the latest versions of files stored in your archive.

If your backup software has a snapshot feature, you should be able to select your most recent update and restore all the files from that date to their original locations. If your software uses *differential* additive archives, you must first restore the original, full archive backup and then restore the files from the most recent update.

If your backup software creates additive incremental archives—but without a snapshot feature—you must again start by restoring the original, full archive backup. Then, step through each day's update, copying its files into their original locations (overwriting the older versions). Depending on how many files have changed and how long it's been since your last backup, this could be a lengthy process.

Note: If you've chosen to maintain a full archive and your archive backup was updated more recently than your duplicate was, you may opt to restore your archive directly. To restore a full archive:

1. Start up from your duplicate disk.

2. Using Disk Utility, erase your internal disk.

3. Select the icon for the internal disk in the Finder and choose File > Get Info. In the Ownership & Permissions section of the window, make sure Ignore Ownership on This Volume is *deselected*.

4. Open your backup software, and use its Restore feature to copy the archived files (as of their most recent backup) to the internal disk.

5. Use the Startup Disk pane of System Preferences to set your internal disk as the startup volume, and restart the computer.

Your Mac should boot properly from the freshly restored archive. (If it does not, follow the procedure outlined previously to restore your duplicate, and then restore your newer archived files.

Appendix A
Troubleshooting Resources

I wish I could promise you that by following the suggestions in this book, you'll never experience any problems with your Mac. You will lessen the likelihood and perhaps the severity of problems, but things still can and will go wrong. If, when an application crashes, your hard disk won't mount or smoke starts pouring out of your SuperDrive, you need more help than I can give you here. But allow me to suggest some places you might look for solutions.

Web sites:

♦ **Apple's support site:** Your first stop should be Apple's official support site, where you can search for FAQs, technical notes, and downloads that may address your problem (www.apple.com/support/).

♦ **Apple's discussion forums:** Another Mac user may have discovered, and solved, a similar problem. Connect with other users at these forums (http://discussions.apple.com/).

♦ **MacFixIt:** Check the MacFixIt site daily for information about newly identified problems and solutions for all sorts of Mac hardware and software (www.macfixit.com).

- **MacInTouch:** Keep current with Mac news and real-world reports from users around the world (www.macintouch.com).

- **MacOSXHints:** This site is geared more toward tips and tricks than troubleshooting, but it does contain solutions to many unusual problems as well (www.macosxhints.com).

- **Software update sites:** VersionTracker (www.versiontracker.com) and MacUpdate (www.macupdate.com) provide up-to-the-minute information on updates for thousands of applications, along with user comments.

Printed books:

- *Mac OS X Help Line, Tiger Edition,* by Ted Landau and Dan Frakes, contains a wealth of troubleshooting and repair information (www.amazon.com/gp/product/0321334299/; $50 retail, Amazon.com price $33).

Ebooks:

- *Troubleshooting Mac OS X,* by "Dr. Smoke" (Gregory A. Swain), is a 600-page ebook that goes into great detail about solving a wide variety of Mac problems (www.thexlab.com/book/troubleshootingmacosx.html; $20).

When all else fails:

- Visit the Genius Bar at a nearby Apple Store for free advice; Apple Stores also offer expert repair services. Be sure to call ahead (or visit the store's Web site; see www.apple.com/retail/) to make an appointment.

- If you're not near an Apple Store, search for an Apple Authorized Service Provider (www.apple.com/buy/locator/service.html).

Appendix B
Backup Software

This appendix includes further information on the backup software mentioned in this book. These lists are not exhaustive, and backup software is updated frequently. By the time you read this, any of these applications might have gained new features, possibly even putting it into an entirely different category. So, before making a purchase, check the developer's Web site for current features and prices. In many cases, you can download a free, time-limited demo to try the software out before making a purchase.

Duplication+Archiving Software

The following applications offer both duplication and archiving features. **Table 3**, "Duplication+Archiving Software Feature Comparison," provides further detail about each one.

Backup Simplicity 3.0 (www.qdea.com; $50)

Data Backup 2.1 (www.prosofteng.com; $59)

Déjà Vu 3.2 (propagandaprod.com; $25)

Personal Backup X4 (www.intego.com; $70)

Retrospect Desktop 6.1 (www.emcinsignia.com; downloadable, $119; boxed, $129; upgrade from Express, $55)

Retrospect Express (www.emcinsignia.com; free with selected third-party hard drives; also included in Allume's $99 CheckIt bundle, www.allume.com/mac/checkit/)

RsyncX 2.1 (http://archive.macosxlabs.org/rsyncx/; free)

Synchronize Pro X 5.0 (www.qdea.com; $100)

Synk Pro 6, Synk Standard, Synk Backup (www.decimus.net; $45, $35, and $25 respectively)

Tri-Backup 4.0 (www.tri-edre.com; $49)

Table 3: Duplication+Archiving Software Feature Comparison

		Backup Simplicity	Data Backup	Déjà Vu	Personal Backup X	Retrospect Desktop	Retrospect Express	RsyncX	Synchronize Pro X	Synk Pro	Tri-Backup
Targets	Hard Disk	Yes	Yes	Yes	Yes	Yes	Yes	Yes	[1]	[1]	[1]
	Disk Image	[1]	[1]	[1]	[1]	[1]	[1]	[1]	[1]	[1]	[1]
	CD/DVD	[2]	[2]	[2]	[2]	Yes	Yes	[2]	[2]	[2]	[2]
	♦ Multisession	No	No	No	No	[9]	[9]	No	No	No	No
	♦ Media Spanning	No	No	[7]	Yes	Yes	Yes	No	No	No	[14]
	Network Servers	No	Yes	Yes	Yes	Yes	Yes	Yes	Yes	Yes	Yes
Archives	Additive Incremental	[3]	[6]	Yes	No	Yes	Yes	[12]	Yes	Yes	[15]
	Rotating Archives	No	Yes	Yes	No	No	No	No	Yes	Yes	Yes
	Rotating Backups	No	No	No	Yes	No	No	Yes	No	No	Yes
	Snapshots	No	Yes	No	No	Yes	Yes	[13]	No	No	Yes
	File List	No	No	Yes	No	[10]	[10]	No	No	No	No
	Selectors	No	No	No	No	Yes	Yes	No	No	Yes	Yes
	Exclusions	[4]	Yes	No	Yes	Yes	[4]	No	Yes	Yes	Yes
Other	Compression	No	Yes	No	[8]	Yes	Yes	Yes	[7]	Yes	Yes
	Encryption	No	Yes	No	Yes	Yes	Yes	[7]	[7]	Yes	Yes
	Restore Feature	Yes	Yes	No	Yes	Yes	Yes	No	No	No	Yes
	Client-Server	No	No	No	No	Yes	No	Yes	No	No	No
Notes		[5]				[11]	[11]				

[1] Only if created by user.

[2] Only if mounted in the Finder.

[3] /Users folder only.

[4] Limited.

[5] Can only back up startup volume.

[6] Yes; "Versioned Backup."

[7] Toast includes a bundled version of Déjà Vu that supports media spanning.

[8] Only for disk images.

[9] Packet-writing support for adding data to partly-used optical discs.

[10] Searchable.

[11] Backup Server function.

[12] What RsyncX calls "Rotating Backups" are actually additive incremental archives.

[13] RsyncX's incremental archives function as their own snapshots.

[14] Manual only.

[15] Yes; "Evolutive Mirror Backup."

Duplication Software

Applications in this group offer duplication (and, in some cases, synchronization) capabilities but not archiving. Because they are so similar in terms of this single feature, I don't provide a comparison table. With the exception of Clone'X and MimMac, all these applications offer scheduled duplication.

BounceBack Professional 7.0 (www.cmsproducts.com; $79)

Carbon Copy Cloner 2.3 (www.bombich.com/software/ccc.html; free; $5 donation suggested)

Clone'X 2.0 (www.tri-edre.com; $49)

CopyCatX III (www.SubRosaSoft.com; download only, $50; CD, $60)

FoldersSynchronizer 3.6 (www.softobe.com; $40)

MimMac 1.8 (www.ascendantsoft.com; $10)

SilverKeeper 1.1 (www.lacie.com/silverkeeper/; free)

QuickBack 3.0, part of SpeedTools Utilities (www.speedtools.com; $90)

SuperDuper! 2.1 (www.shirt-pocket.com; $28; free "clone-only" version available)

Xupport 3.0 (www.computer-support.ch/xupport/; $20)

Archiving Software

These programs offer archiving (and, in some cases, synchronization) features and scheduled backups, but they cannot make bootable duplicates. **Table 4,** "Archiving Software Feature Comparison," provides more detail about each application.

Apple Backup 3.1 (www.mac.com; free with $100 .Mac subscription)

Archive Assistant, part of StuffIt Deluxe 10.0 (www.stuffit.com; $80)

BackupSW 3.4 (visualversion.com/backupsw/; $9)

BRU LE 1.2 (www.bru.com/products/macosx/le/; $129)

ChronoSync[2] **3.3** (www.econtechnologies.com; $30)

Dobry Backuper 1.5 (dobrysoft.com; $30)

NTI Shadow[3] **3** (www.ntius.com; $30)

SwitchBack 3.9 (www.glendower.co.nz; $30)

SyncupX 1.6 (http://freeridecoding.net/syncupx/; $20)

---

[2]   Can be coaxed into making duplicates, but the publisher discourages this usage.

[3]   In addition to manual and scheduled backups, NTI Shadow can add files to an archive every single time they're saved.

Table 4: Archiving Software Feature Comparison

		Apple Backup 3	Archive Assistant	BackupSW	BRU LE	ChronoSync	Dobry Backuper	NTI Shadow	SwitchBack	SyncupX
Targets	Hard Disk	Yes	Yes	Yes	Yes	Yes	Yes	Yes	Yes	Yes
	Disk Image	[1]	[3]	[3]	[3]	[3]	[3]	[3]	[3]	[3]
	CD/DVD	Yes	Yes	[4]	[4]	[4]	Yes	[4]	[4]	[4]
	◆ Multisession	No	No	No	No	No	No	No	No	No
	◆ Media Spanning	Yes	Yes	No	Yes	No	Yes	No	No	No
	Network Servers	Yes	Yes	Yes	Yes	Yes	Yes	Yes	Yes	Yes
Archives	Additive Incremental	Yes	Yes	Yes	[6]	Yes	Yes	Yes	Yes	Yes
	Rotating Archives	No	No	No	No	Yes	No	Yes	No	No
	Rotating Backups	No	No	No	No	No	Yes	No	No	No
	Snapshots	Yes	No	No	No	No	[8]	No	No	No
	File List	No	No	Yes	Yes	[8]	Yes	No	No	No
	Selectors	Yes	Yes	Yes	Yes	Yes	No	Yes	No	No
	Exclusions	[2]	Yes	Yes	Yes	Yes	Yes	Yes	Yes	Yes
Other	Compression	Yes	Yes	Yes	Yes	No	Yes	No	No	No
	Encryption	No	Yes	No	No	No	No	No	No	No
	Restore Feature	Yes	Yes	Yes	Yes	[8]	Yes	No	No	Yes
	Client-Server	No	No	Yes	No	No	No	No	No	No
Notes				[5]	[7]		[9]			[10]

[1] Although Backup's archives are based on disk images, you can store them on other disk images only if they're mounted in the Finder.

[2] Manual only.

[3] Only if created by user.

[4] Only if mounted in the Finder.

[5] Awkward, un-Mac-like interface.

[6] Only for tapes.

[7] Optimized for tape drives.

[8] Limited.

[9] Uses the term "versioned" to refer to rotating backups.

[10] Uses iCal for scheduling.

Synchronization Software

The following utilities provide either one-way or two-way synchronization of files and folders. Because they offer neither duplicates nor archives in the sense discussed in this book, I do not categorize them as true backup software.

AASync 1.2 (www.aasync.com; two versions: one free, one $19)

iBackup 5.0 (www.grapefruit.ch/iBackup/; free)

iMsafe 2.0 (http://homepage.mac.com/sweetcocoa/; $19)

iShelter 1.0 (www.brattoo.com/propaganda/; $10)

Phew 1.0 (www.substancesoftware.com; free)

Synchronize X Plus 3.0 (www.qdea.com; $30)

zsCompare 3.0 (www.zizasoft.com; $35)

Photo-Cataloging Software

iView MediaPro (www.iview-multimedia.com; $160)

Extensis Portfolio (www.extensis.com; $200)

Photo-Sharing Services

Flickr (www.flickr.com; free–$25/year)

Fotki (www.fotki.com; free–$50/year)

Kodak EasyShare Gallery (www.kodakgallery.com; free with annual purchase)

SmugMug (www.smugmug.com; $30–100/year)

Snapfish (www.snapfish.com; free with annual purchase)

Internet Backup Services

These services include proprietary software. After subscribing and installing the software, you would be able to perform (limited) backups to a secure server over the Internet.

BackJack (www.backjack.com)

Datatrieve (www.datatrieve.co.uk)

Prolifix (www.prolifix.net)

Tuloy (www.tuloy.com)

Version Control Software

The tools listed here enable you to store unlimited versions of documents from almost any application—in some cases, every time you save a file. Before attempting to use CVS (Concurrent Versions System) software, read "Version Control with CVS on Mac OS X," an introductory article on CVS at http://developer.apple.com/internet/opensource/cvsoverview.html.

MacCvs (http://cvsgui.sourceforge.net/; free)

MacCVSClient (www.heilancoo.net/MacCVSClient/; free; contributions accepted)

MacCVS Pro (www.maccvs.org; free)

Subversion (http://subversion.tigris.org/; free)

VOODOO Server (www.unisoftwareplus.com/products/voodooserver/; server license, $79; remote client license, $129)

darcs (http://darcs.darwinports.com/; free)

Other Software

DV Backup 1.4 (http://coolatoola.com/; $50; Lite version, $20)

Appendix C
A Retrospect Primer

Throughout this book, I've sung the praises of Retrospect, the well-known backup software from EMC Insignia (formerly from Dantz). It's my main backup tool (though I do use other software for certain tasks). Although I've tried every backup program I can get my hands on, I haven't encountered anything that impressed me enough to tempt me away from Retrospect.

And yet, I'm well aware—believe me—of Retrospect's shortcomings. I get email all the time from people who find it inscrutable. I've read many complaints about Retrospect on Web sites and discussion lists. And I've encountered numerous problems myself. But although Retrospect surely has some bugs and limitations, its biggest problem is the user interface. It's weird. It's confusing. It's 10 years overdue for an extreme makeover. And the difficulty ordinary users have in getting past the interface to the useful stuff beneath is the main reason so many people are looking for alternatives to Retrospect.

When I started using Retrospect way back when, I found it confusing, too. Its 250+ page manual contains plenty of helpful information, but it's a lot to get one's brain around. With some effort, though, I managed to figure out enough of Retrospect to get my own backups working, and eventually

I became so accustomed to the interface that I barely notice how weird it is anymore.

In the next few pages, I provide a brief overview of Retrospect's terminology, logic, and interface—with special attention to things you're likely to find confusing. I won't cover everything, of course, but I hope I can give enough information that you can feel comfortable using it for basic duplicates and archives—for a single computer or for a small network. Unless otherwise noted, everything in this appendix applies to both Retrospect Desktop and Retrospect Express.

Retrospect Terminology

Before I get into specific Retrospect windows or activities, I want to explain some important terms as Retrospect uses them. Understanding these words will make everything else much easier.

♦ **Backup:** An operation in which Retrospect copies files into a special file called a backup set (see "Backup Set," ahead in this list). Every backup to a given backup set after the first one is, by definition, an additive incremental archive. (Retrospect doesn't perform differential backups.) So, for the remainder of this appendix, I use the term "backup" to refer to what I normally call an "archive."

♦ **Duplicate:** An operation in which the entire contents of a volume are copied *exactly* to another volume. Subsequent duplicates are incremental, and may delete files absent on the source (using the "Replace Entire Disk" option) or leave such files on the destination (using the "Replace Corresponding Files" option). Duplicates of startup volumes to external FireWire drives, secondary internal drives, or partitions on such drives, should be bootable—as long as you chose the "Replace Entire Disk" option. Duplicates do not use backup sets.

♦ **Archive:** A backup operation in which Retrospect deletes the original files after copying them into a backup set.

♦ **Restore:** An operation in which files are copied from a backup set to another location—which may or may not be their original location.

- **Script:** A saved set of options for a backup, duplicate, archive, or restore operation, which you can run at any time (manually or on a schedule). Scripts include what data you're backing up, to what destination, with which selectors and other options, and schedule information. The term "Script" is a bit of a misnomer—unlike with AppleScript scripts, shell scripts, and so on, you don't actually see a *script* (a sequence of coded instructions); you see only settings in dialogs and windows.

- **Backup Server:** A script type for backups (not found in Retrospect Express) that provides for a flexible schedule and multiple backup sets. Using this script type, Retrospect can back up clients whenever they happen to be available on the network, and store the backups on whatever media happens to be present. This makes backing up laptops and rotating backup media much easier.

- **EasyScript:** A series of dialogs that walk you through the creation of a basic backup script (including a Backup Set, if necessary) by asking you simple questions. I've found that EasyScript selections always require significant modification after the fact, so I prefer to skip EasyScript and define my own scripts manually.

- **Backup Set:** A special file that stores all the files and folders you're backing up; what I refer to elsewhere in this book as an *archive*. A backup set can contain many versions of any given file, and may optionally be compressed, encrypted, or both. Backup sets are readable only by Retrospect; you can't access their contents directly from the Finder.

- **Catalog:** An index of a backup set's contents. For backup sets stored on a hard disk or network server, you can opt to store the catalog in the same file as the backup set or as a separate file (even on a different volume from the backup set), so you can view and search the contents of your backups even if the backup set itself is unavailable. (Backup sets stored on removable media always keep their catalog files on your hard disk.) If a catalog is missing or damaged, Retrospect can reconstruct it from the backup set itself.

- **Source:** Whatever you're backing up—volume(s) or subvolume(s) on one or more physical drives.

- **Destination:** The location where backed-up files will be stored. For backup, backup server, and archive operations, the destination must be a backup set (or more than one backup set); for duplicate operations, the destination must be a volume.

- **Subvolume:** A folder you've designated as a backup source or destination. You cannot create a bootable volume by duplicating a startup volume to a subvolume, because as far as Mac OS X is concerned, a subvolume is just a folder.

- **Client:** A computer on your network that's running Retrospect Client, and which you can back up to a server running Retrospect Desktop.

- **Device:** A physical device that can store data—such as an optical drive or a tape drive. (Hard drives and network servers don't count as "devices" in Retrospect's usage.) Some devices require special setup before they can be used, but in most cases, optical drives are recognized automatically.

- **Normal:** The default backup behavior, which is to copy all the selected files on the first run, and then copy only new or changed files (an additive incremental archive) on subsequent runs.

- **Recycle:** This setting instructs Retrospect to erase a backup set and then perform a normal backup.

- **New Media:** This setting instructs Retrospect to create a fresh backup set (with all the attributes of an existing set) on a new set of media, without erasing the existing media.

The Directory

When you open Retrospect, its main window, called the Directory, appears (see **Figure 14**). You can click any of the tab-like buttons at the top of the window to display a pane containing a few buttons; clicking these buttons opens the windows where you actually perform useful tasks. The number and names of these tabs (and the controls on them) differ between Retrospect Desktop and Retrospect Express.

Figure 14

Retrospect's main Directory window. This figure shows Retrospect Desktop; Retrospect Express has fewer panes and a somewhat different arrangement of buttons.

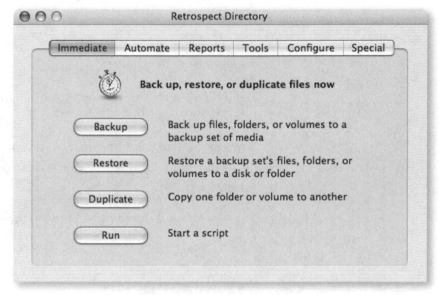

When you click a button to open a window, the Directory usually remains visible in the background; you can return to it at any time by choosing Retrospect Directory (or Retrospect Express Directory) from the Window menu. Be aware that almost every action you perform in Retrospect opens at least one new window; you could easily end up with half a dozen or more windows open at once.

Because Retrospect helpfully includes explanations of each button right in the Directory window, I'm not going to reiterate all the button names and functions here. I do, however, want to point out where you can find some commonly used features.

♦ **To set Retrospect's preferences:** In Retrospect Desktop, click Preferences on the Special pane. In Retrospect Express, click Preferences on the Configure pane.

Note: For most users, Retrospect's default preferences are ideal.

♦ **To set up a recurring Duplicate or Backup:** Click Scripts on the Automate pane. See *Set Up a Duplicate Script* (this page) and *Set Up a Backup Script* (page 203).

♦ **To restore backed-up files:** Click Restore on the Immediate pane. See *Restore a Backup* (page 210).

♦ **To duplicate a volume as a one-time activity:** Click Duplicate on the Immediate pane.

♦ **To prepare client machines on your network for backup:** Click Clients on the Configure pane (Retrospect Desktop only). See *Back Up Network Clients* (page 207).

♦ **To run a script immediately:** Choose the script name from the Run menu.

Set Up a Duplicate Script

In Retrospect, if you want to make a bootable copy of your hard disk, you use the Duplicate feature. You can create a one-off duplicate by clicking Duplicate on the Immediate tab, but here, we're concerned with setting up duplicates as a regularly scheduled activity. To do so, follow these steps:

1. Click the Automate tab, and then click the Scripts button. The Scripts window appears.

2. Click New to create a new script, and select Duplicate in the dialog that appears. Click OK.

3. Enter a name for your script (see *Label Media and Files*, page 162, for suggestions) and click OK. The Duplicate window appears (**Figure 15**).

Figure 15

The Duplicate window, like other script summary windows, provides an overview of the options selected for this script.

Duplicate: My Duplicate

Source   (No volume selected)
Destination   (No volume selected)
Selecting   All Files
Options   Verification on
                Don't backup FileVault sparseimages
Schedule   (Not scheduled)

4. Click the Source button. Select the volume you want to duplicate and click OK.

5. Click the Destination button. Select the volume where your duplicate will be stored. Choose Replace Entire Disk (or Replace Entire Contents) from the pop-up menu at the top of the window—*not* Replace Corresponding Files!—and click OK. Keep in mind that the destination volume, if a hard disk or partition, must be at least as large as the amount of data on the source volume.

Note: You must choose a volume icon—not a subvolume or folder icon—as the destination if you wish your duplicate to be bootable.

Warning! Check to see that the destination volume does not ignore ownership; if it does, your duplicate will not be bootable. To check this, select the destination volume's icon in the Finder and choose File > Get Info. In the Ownership & Permissions portion of the window, make sure the checkbox labeled Ignore Ownership On This Volume is deselected.

6. Optionally, click the Selecting button and make a selection from the pop-up menu to restrict which files are copied. You might, for example, choose All Files Except Cache Files or All Except Cache & Spotlight; these two choices will speed up the duplication while omitting non-critical files. If you're using Retrospect Desktop, you can click More Choices to access more-sophisticated selectors. When you're finished, click OK.

7. Click the Options button. Make sure the Verification checkbox is selected, and click OK.

8. Click the Schedule button and add in your desired schedule. (I talk more about setting up schedules in *Schedule a Duplicate,* ahead.) When you finish, click OK.

9. Close the Duplicate window, and click Save when prompted.

Your Duplicate script is now ready to go, and will run on the schedule you set—even if you quit Retrospect. If you want to run it immediately, choose the script's name from the Run menu.

After testing your duplicate (read *Test Your Duplicate,* page 165), you can repeat this procedure to set up Duplicate scripts for additional hard disks or other media.

Schedule a Duplicate

You can schedule duplicates to occur as frequently or as seldom as you wish, but I suggest running them at least once a week. Better yet, use two or more hard drives and alternate your duplicates between them—drive #1 one week, then drive #2, and so on. This scheme will enable you to keep one of the drives off-site at all times. In this example, I show how to schedule duplicates to run once a week, alternating between two drives. Feel free to alter these instructions to meet your needs if you're using a different number of drives or want to run duplicates at a different frequency.

To schedule an alternating weekly duplicate in Retrospect, follow these steps:

1. Select the Automate tab and click the Scripts button.

2. Select the Duplicate script that you created for your first drive; then click Edit.

3. Click the Schedule button, and then the Add button (**Figure 16**).

Figure 16

Retrospect's Schedule list (still empty in this example) appears when you click the Schedule button for a script. Add a new schedule by clicking the Add button in this dialog.

4. For the kind of schedule to add, choose Repeating Interval.

5. Enter today's date as the start date.

6. Choose the day of the week on which you want the backup to occur, and select a time.

7. From the Repeat pop-up menu, choose Every <x> Weeks on <day of week>.

8. In the field labeled Weeks, enter 2 if you have two sets of media or 3 if you have three sets of media. **Figure 17** on the next page shows an example of what the finished schedule may look like.

9. Confirm that the text at the top of the dialog matches your expectations, as in "Do Duplicate Every other week on Wednesday, starting 12/01/2005 at 2:00 AM." Then click OK.

10. Select your next Duplicate script and repeat Steps 3–8, but in Step 4, choose a start date 1 week later.

Your selected scripts will now alternate on a weekly basis.

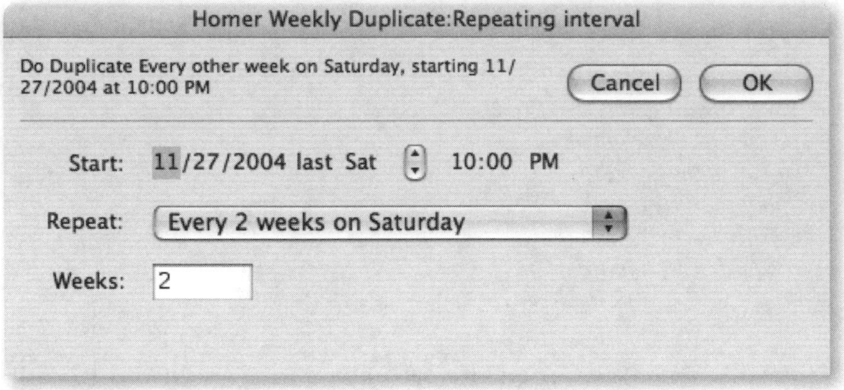

Figure 17

This repeating interval schedule in Retrospect runs every 2 weeks on Saturday. To change it to every 3 weeks, enter 3 in the Weeks field; to change the interval from weeks to days or months, use the Repeat pop-up menu.

Note: After you set up a schedule, you can quit Retrospect. Retrospect installs a small background application in your /Library/StartupItems folder called RetroRun, which monitors your scheduled backups and launches Retrospect, when necessary, to run them at the proper times.

Set Up a Backup Server Script

Backup Server is a wonderful feature—actually a script type, which can make rotating archives incredibly easy. (Unfortunately, it cannot be used for duplicates.) Backup Server has two main attributes:

♦ It constantly polls all designated sources (which could be a folder on a local volume or another computer on your network) to see if they've been backed up within the past 24 hours—or whatever interval you choose—and if not, it performs a backup immediately. (You can also restrict the Backup Server to run only during certain times of certain days.) This way, even if your laptop is not available for daily backups on a fixed schedule, you can be sure backups will occur when it is present.

♦ It uses any designated media that happens to be available at the moment. So you could set up three different hard drives as backup destinations, attach or detach them whenever you like, and Retrospect automatically updates the oldest archive available the next time it runs. This eliminates the need to maintain a strict schedule for swapping media to take it off-site.

If you're using Retrospect Desktop, Backup Server is generally a much better choice for automated archives than a fixed schedule. (This feature is absent in Retrospect Express, so if you're using Express, or wish to follow a fixed schedule, see *Set Up a Backup Script,* page 203.)

To use Retrospect's Backup Server feature, follow these steps:

1. Click the Automate tab, and then click the Scripts button.

2. In the Scripts window that appears, click New to create a new script, and choose Backup Server in the dialog that appears (**Figure 18**).

Figure 18

To use Retrospect's Backup Server feature, select it as the script type in this dialog.

3. Enter a name for your script (see *Label Media and Files,* page 162, for suggestions) and click OK. The Backup Server window appears.

4. Click the Source button to display the Volume Selection window. To back up an entire volume, select it in here. To back up just *part* of a volume, select the volume and click Subvolume. Navigate to a folder you'd like to back up (such as your home folder) and click Define. You can repeat this as many times as necessary. Each subvolume you define then appears as a folder in the Volume Selection window. (To select multiple volumes or subvolumes in this window, hold down Command while clicking.) When you're finished selecting sources, click OK.

5. Click the Destination button. *Two* dialogs open: the Destinations dialog and, in front of that, the Backup Set Selection dialog. You should add backup sets for each of the drives you're using to store your archives. If you've already defined the backup set(s) you want to use, select them here (Command-click to select more than one backup set). If not, follow these steps:

   a. Click New to create a new backup set.

   b. Choose File (*not* Removable Disk!) from the Backup Set Type pop-up menu.

   c. If you want to encrypt the backup set, click the Secure button, select an encryption type, and enter a passphrase.

   Note: You must decide whether to use encryption when you initially create a backup set. You can't change the encryption settings for a backup set after the fact.

   ---

   d. Give your backup set a descriptive name and click New.

   e. Select the volume (normally an external hard disk) where you want to store the backup set and click Save.

   f. Repeat Steps a–e, if necessary, for additional backup sets; then, select the set(s) you want to use and click OK.

   When you've finished adding backup sets to the script, click OK to dismiss the Destinations dialog.

6. Optionally, click the Selecting button and make a selection from the pop-up menu to restrict which files are copied. You might, for example, choose All Files Except Cache Files or All Except Cache & Spotlight; these two choices will speed up the backup while omitting non-critical files. You can click More Choices to access more-sophisticated selectors. When you're finished, click OK.

7. Click the Options button. Enter the maximum frequency for your backups—such as "every 1 day" or "every 4 hours." If you want to turn on compression (a good idea), click More Choices, then select Backup in

the list on the left and select the Backup Compression (In Software) checkbox. Click OK.

8. To restrict Backup Server to certain days or times, click the Schedule button. Select the Custom Schedule radio button, and then click Custom. Select the times and days you want the Backup Server to run, then click OK. Finally, click OK a second time to dismiss the Schedule window, and close the Backup Server window.

Backup Server is now configured to archive your files onto the selected backup media whenever they are available. To activate the Backup Server script immediately, choose Run > Start Backup Server. When Backup Server is running, the main Retrospect Directory disappears and the Backup Server window appears instead. To return to the Directory (to make other changes in Retrospect), you must close the Backup Server window and confirm that you really do want to stop the execution of the Backup Server.

Set Up a Backup Script

If you own Retrospect Express and therefore can't use the Backup Server script type—or if you simply prefer to have your backups run on a regular schedule—you should set up a Backup script to perform additive incremental archives. The instructions are similar to those for the Backup Server script, just previously, except that you must specify an explicit schedule.

To set up a Backup script, follow these steps:

1. Click the Automate tab, and then click the Scripts button. The Scripts window appears.

2. Click New to create a new script, and choose Backup in the dialog that appears.

3. Enter a name for your script (see *Label Media and Files,* page 162, for suggestions) and click OK. The Backup window appears.

4. Click the Source button to display the Volume Selection window. To back up an entire volume, select it in this window. To back up just *part* of a volume, select the volume and click Subvolume. Navigate to

a folder you'd like to back up (such as your home folder) and click Define. You can repeat this as many times as necessary. Each subvolume you define then appears as a folder in the Volume Selection window. (To select multiple volumes or subvolumes in this window, hold down Command while clicking.) When you're finished selecting sources, click OK.

5. Click the Destination button. *Two* dialogs open: the Destinations dialog and, in front of that, the Backup Set Selection dialog. Ordinarily, you'll select just one backup set here (and then create an entirely new backup script for each additional destination drive). If you've already defined the backup set you want to use, select it here. If not, follow these steps:

   a. Click New to create a new backup set.

   b. Choose File (*not* Removable Disk!) from the Backup Set Type pop-up menu.

   c. If you want to encrypt the backup set, click the Secure button, select an encryption type, and enter a passphrase.

   Note: You must decide whether to use encryption when you initially create a backup set. You can't change the encryption settings for a backup set after the fact.

   ---

   d. Give your backup set a descriptive name and click New.

   e. Select the volume (normally an external hard disk) where you want to store the backup set and click Save.

   f. Select the set you want to use and click OK.

   When you've added your backup set to the script, click OK to dismiss the Destinations dialog.

6. Optionally, click the Selecting button and make a selection from the pop-up menu to restrict which files are copied. You might, for example, choose All Files Except Cache Files or All Except Cache & Spotlight; these two choices will speed up the backup while omitting non-critical

files. If you're using Retrospect Desktop, you can click More Choices to access more-sophisticated selectors. When you finish, click OK.

7. Click the Options button. Make sure the Verification checkbox is selected, and if you want to turn on compression (a good idea), select the Backup Compression (In Software) checkbox. Click OK.

8. Click the Schedule button and set your schedule. (For more details about setting up schedules, see *Schedule Backups,* just ahead.) When you finish, click OK.

9. Close the Backup window, and click Save when prompted to do so.

Your Backup script is now ready to go, and will run on the schedule you set—even if you quit Retrospect. If you want to run it immediately, choose the script's name from the Run menu.

After testing your archive (see *Test Your Archive,* page 169), you can repeat this procedure to set up Backup scripts for additional hard disks or other media.

Note: Execution Errors. After Retrospect completes a backup, it may display a window saying there were execution errors. Don't worry about this. No, really: *don't worry about it.* Execution errors are common and don't necessarily indicate a problem. Most frequently, an "error" means that something didn't match between Retrospect's pre-backup scan and its post-backup verification, which will be the case if files (such as temporary system files) change while the backup is in progress—which they often do.

Schedule Backups

You can schedule backups to occur as frequently or as seldom as you wish, but I suggest running them at least once a day. Better yet, use two or more hard drives and alternate your backups between them on a weekly basis—drive #1 every day one week, then drive #2 every day the following week, and so on. This sort of scheme enables you to keep one of the drives off-site at all times. In this example, I show how to schedule backups to run daily, alternating between two drives on a weekly basis. Feel free to alter these instructions to meet your needs if you're using a different number of drives or want to run duplicates at a different frequency.

To schedule your backups scripts, follow these steps:

1. Select the Automate tab and click Scripts.

2. Select your first Backup script, and then click Edit.

3. Click the Schedule button, then the Add button.

4. For the kind of schedule to add, choose Day of Week.

5. Enter today's date as the start date.

6. Select the days of the week on which you want the backup to occur, (usually all of them) and select a time.

7. In the field labeled Weeks, enter 2 if you have two sets of media or 3 if you have three sets of media (**Figure 19**).

Figure 19

This Day of Week schedule in Retrospect runs every day for a week, in alternating weeks. To change it to alternate every 3 weeks (if you use three sets of backup media), enter 3 in the Weeks field.

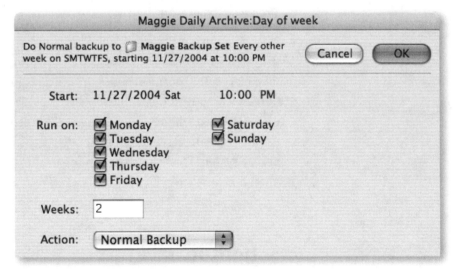

8. Choose Normal Backup from the Action pop-up menu.

9. Confirm that the text at the top of the dialog matches your expectations, as in "Do Normal backup to Maggie Backup Set Every other week on SMTWTFS, starting 11/27/2004 at 10:00 PM." Then click OK.

10. Select your next Backup script and repeat Steps 3–8, but in Step 4, choose a start date 1 week later.

Your selected scripts will now run daily, but alternate on a weekly basis.

Tip: If you have an old Mac (or, say, a Mac mini) that you'd like to turn into a dedicated backup server, read my article "Turn your old Mac into a backup server" in the September 2005 issue of *Macworld:* www.macworld.com/2005/08/features/oldmacnewtricks1/.

Back Up Network Clients

Retrospect Desktop is capable of backing up the machine it's running on, plus up to three other client machines. (You can purchase additional client licenses—or, for larger groups, upgrade to Retrospect Workgroup or Retrospect Server.) This means you can use just one set of backup media and one schedule for several computers, instead of setting up a backup system on each one individually. All you have to do is install Retrospect Client on each client machine, add the clients to Retrospect's list, and select the volumes or subvolumes you want to back up on each one.

The first part of the process is to set up the clients. Follow these steps:

1. On a client machine, install Retrospect Client (the installer is included with Retrospect Desktop).

2. At the end of the installation process, the installer asks you for a password. Choose something different from your standard Mac OS X password—it need not be particularly secure—and confirm it when prompted.

3. The installer then asks if you want to enable a firewall exception for Retrospect. If Mac OS X's firewall is turned on, be sure to answer Yes.

4. Click the installer's Restart button to restart your computer.

5. Open the Retrospect Client application and make sure the On radio button is selected.

Repeat these steps for each client machine. That's it—your clients are now ready to go. The rest of the process happens on the server machine. To configure the server, follow these steps:

1. Open Retrospect Desktop, go to the Configure pane, and click the Clients button.

2. Click the Network button to display a window listing all the clients Retrospect can find on your local network (these are machines with Retrospect Client installed and turned on which are within the same subnet—and not blocked by a firewall). You should have TCP/IP selected as the Network Protocol, and Mac OS X selected as the Type.

Tip: If the machine you're using as a server has a firewall turned on, you must also add an exception for Retrospect. Go to the Firewall tab of the Sharing pane of System Preferences, click New, and choose Retrospect from the Port Name pop-up menu. If it does not appear in the menu, choose Other and enter 497 in the TCP Port Number(s) field.

---

3. If the client you want to add appears in the list, select its name. If the client does not appear in the list, click Add by Address and enter the IP address of the client computer; then, select the client's name in the list. Click Log In, and type in the password you specified when you set up that client. Also confirm (or modify) the name for the client as it will appear in the server's lists. Repeat this step as necessary for additional clients.

4. After adding a client, the Client Configuration dialog should appear. (If it does not, double-click the client name in the Backup Client Database window.) On the General pane of this dialog, select Link Encryption if the client is connecting over a wireless network, or you want to add extra security to the data as it travels between the client and the server. From the Backup pop-up menu, choose Selected Volumes.

5. On the Volumes pane, select all the volumes from the client machine that contain files or folders you want to back up. Click OK. Repeat as necessary for additional clients, and close the Backup Client Database window.

Now your clients are ready to be added to your backup scripts. Follow the instructions in *Set Up a Duplicate Script* (page 196), *Set Up a Backup Server Script* (page 200), or *Set Up a Backup Script* (page 203) to add clients to your scripts; the volume(s) you selected in Step 5 will appear in the Sources lists, and you can define subvolumes and selectors just as you did for items on the server itself.

Tip: If you're making *duplicates* of clients over the network, remember to choose a volume—not a subvolume!—as the destination. You'll probably want to store each duplicate on a separate FireWire hard drive, or at least a separate *partition* of a FireWire hard drive, so that you can later attach that drive to the client machine if you need to boot from the duplicate.

Recycle a Backup Set

If you're storing your archives on hard disks, they will eventually fill up. How long that takes depends on the size of the disks, whether or not you use compression, and how frequently your files change. If the disk holding a backup set becomes completely full, Retrospect will continue attempting to run your backup scripts, but each one will fail due to a lack of disk space. Therefore, you should check on your free space periodically and, when it begins to get low, recycle your media—in other words, erase the backup set and start over with a full backup.

The procedure to do so is easy, but it isn't obvious. To recycle a backup set, follow these steps:

1. On the Configure pane, click the Backup Sets button. The Backup Sets window appears.

2. Select the backup set you want to recycle—the one that's stored on whichever volume is closest to being full. Click Configure. A new dialog opens.

3. Click the Options tab. At the bottom of the Options pane is a Media section with a single button: Action. Click the Action button. The Media Control Manual Override dialog appears.

4. Select the Recycle radio button and click OK. This tells Retrospect that for the *next* run of this script only, it should use the Recycle action—erase the backup set and then perform a full backup.

5. Close all the other windows, saving your changes if prompted.

The next time your backup script runs, it will recycle that backup set.

Needless to say, when you recycle a backup set, you lose all the old incremental archives from that set. Therefore, you should not recycle if you've had any computer problems recently that make you suspect you'll need to access older versions of your files! The best practice, assuming you have more than one backup set for your archives, is to stagger their recycling dates—by a month or more, if possible. That way, you'll always have at least several older copies of your files.

Restore a Backup

Retrospect's Restore feature can sometimes be confusing. But don't panic. When you need to recover backed-up files, follow the instructions here that most closely match your situation.

Whichever method you choose, remember that Retrospect treats Restore operations in a method very similar to Backup or Duplicate operations—you choose the Source (the volume or backup set containing the files you want to restore), the Destination (where to put the restored files), and various Options. You also, in some cases, choose particular files within the Source that you want to recover. Then perform the actual restoration.

Restore a Duplicate

Before restoring a duplicate, consider whether that's really what you want to do. Remember that you can boot your computer from a duplicate (as long as it's stored on its own volume on a FireWire hard drive or, if you're using an Intel Mac, a USB drive). If your internal disk has problems, you may find that you can boot from the duplicate and then run a utility to repair your internal disk. That can save you some time and effort over restoring the duplicate.

Note: If you want to boot from a duplicate you created over a network, either physically connect the hard drive it's on (internally or via FireWire) to the client machine, or restore the duplicate onto the client's hard drive over the network. You can't boot from a duplicate over a network.

However, if disk repair doesn't work (or if, for any other reason, you want to restore a duplicate, in its entirety, to the original volume), do *not* use Retrospect's Restore command! The Restore feature is only for files stored in backup sets (that is, archives). Instead, click the Duplicate button on the Immediate pane. Follow the same procedure you used for creating your duplicate, only swap the Source and Destination drives. Retrospect will then copy your duplicate back onto its original volume.

Restore the Entire Contents of a Backup

If you've been archiving files to a backup set using a backup script and you want to replace the *entire* set of files on your original volume with the backed-up copies (whether the most recent snapshot or not), follow these steps:

1. On the Immediate pane, click the Restore button. A dialog appears.

2. Select the Restore an Entire Disk radio button (yes, even if you didn't back up your entire disk) and click OK. The Restore from Backup: Source dialog appears.

3. Select the backup set containing the files you want to restore. If you've backed up to multiple backup sets on different drives, you'll generally want to select the backup set with the most recent date.

4. When you select a backup set, the bottom portion of the window displays the most recent snapshot for each of the volumes (or sub-volumes) in that set. If you want to restore files from the most recent snapshot, simply select the volume you want to restore in this list. However, if you want to restore the files as they appeared at an earlier time, click Add Snapshot. The Snapshot Retrieval window appears, listing snapshots for every backup session stored in this backup set.

Select the one you want and click Retrieve. Then, select that snapshot in the Restore from Backup: Source dialog and click OK.

5. In the Destination Selection dialog that appears, select the original volume or subvolume corresponding to the snapshot you selected in Step 4. Make sure the pop-up menu at the top of the window says Replace Entire Disk (the default setting), and click OK. When the confirmation alert appears, click Replace.

    Warning! *Although it should be obvious by now, you are about to overwrite the files on your hard disk with the ones from your backup. If you are not completely certain this is what you want to do, select a* different *destination in Step 5 and then manually move the files to their original locations.*

6. After a few minutes of file scanning, Retrospect displays the Restore from Backup summary window. This is your last chance to make changes to your source, destination, or options before restoring your files. When you're ready to go for it, click Restore.

Retrospect restores all the files from your selected snapshot to their original locations.

Restore Individual Files or Folders from a Backup

Most of the time when I dip into an archive, it's to find an older version of a particular file or folder I inadvertently modified or deleted. These situations fall into two categories. In the first case, I know (at least roughly) when the version of the file I'm looking for would have been backed up—and thus, I know which backup set likely contains it. In the second case, the file could be in any of several backup sets, and I'm not certain when a good copy was last backed up. Each situation requires a slightly different procedure.

If you know which backup set contains the files you want and when they were backed up, follow these steps to restore your files:

1. On the Immediate pane, click the Restore button. A dialog appears.

2. Select the Restore Files from a Backup button and click OK. The Restore from Backup: Source dialog appears.

3. Select the backup set containing the files you want to restore. If you've backed up to multiple backup sets on different drives, you'll generally want to select the backup set with the most recent date.

4. When you select a backup set, the bottom portion of the window displays the most recent snapshot for each of the volumes (or subvolumes) in that set. If you want to restore files from the most recent snapshot, simply select the volume you want to restore in this list. However, if you want to restore the files as they appeared at an earlier time, click Add Snapshot. The Snapshot Retrieval window appears, listing snapshots for every backup session stored in this backup set. Select the one you want and click Retrieve. Then, select that snapshot in the Restore from Backup: Source dialog and click OK.

Note: Right now, you're selecting only the *snapshot* containing the files or folders you want to restore. Later, in Step 7, you'll narrow that down to particular files or folders.

---

5. In the Destination Selection dialog that appears, select the volume or subvolume where you want to put the restored files. Although you can choose the original location, a safer option is to leave the existing copies of the files and folders (if any) alone and restore the backups to another location. Make sure the pop-up menu at the top of the window says Retrieve Files & Folders (the default setting), and click OK.

6. After a few minutes of file scanning, Retrospect displays the Restore from Backup summary window. To select the files and folders you want to restore, click the Files Chosen button. A window appears listing all the files in the snapshot you selected.

7. In the snapshot list, navigate to the file(s) or folder(s) you want to restore. Double-click an item (or select it and click the Mark button at the top of the window) to indicate that you want to restore it. (A checkmark appears next to each file selected for restoration.) Repeat for as many items as you wish. When you finish selecting files, close the window.

8. Back in the Restore from Backup summary window, click Restore.

Retrospect copies the items you marked to the specified destination. It maintains the original folder structure, so what you'll see if you look in the destination location is a folder with the same name as your backup set. Inside that folder will normally be another series of folders mirroring the original folder hierarchy, and if you navigate down through these folders, you'll find the files you just restored.

If you're unsure where the files you want are located or when they were backed up, follow these steps to restore your files:

1. On the Immediate pane, click the Restore button. A dialog appears.

2. Select the Search for Files and Folders button and click OK. The Restore from Backup: Source dialog appears.

3. Select one or more backup sets—if you have no idea where your files may be, select all the backup sets. Then click OK.

4. In the Destination Selection dialog that appears, select the volume or subvolume where you want to put the restored files. Although you can choose the original location, a safer option is to leave the existing copies of the files and folders (if any) alone and restore the backups to another location. Make sure the pop-up menu at the top of the window says Retrieve Files & Folders (the default setting), and click OK.

5. Retrospect displays the Searching & Retrieval dialog. Use the pop-up menus to specify search criteria (just as you would in a Finder search) and click OK. Retrospect searches through the selected backup set(s) and selects all matching files.

6. The Searching & Retrieval summary window appears. In the Files Chosen section, the window lists the total number of matching files it found.

7. If you want to narrow that list down further to just particular files, click the Files Chosen button. In the list that appears, double-click an item (or select it and click the Unmark button at the top of the window) to indicate that you want to exclude it from the restoration. (A checkmark appears next to each file selected for restoration.) Repeat for as many

items as you wish. When you finish selecting or deselecting files, close the window.

8. In the Searching & Retrieval summary window, click Retrieve.

Retrospect copies the items you marked to the specified destination. It maintains the original folder structure, so what you'll see if you look in the destination location is a folder with the same name as your backup set. Inside that folder will normally be another series of folders that mirror the original folder hierarchy, and if you navigate down through these folders, you'll find the files you just restored.

Glossary

additive: When a backup copies files that are new, renamed, or modified since the last session without deleting or overwriting older versions, that backup (normally an archive) is additive.

additive incremental archive: A type of backup in which files that are new or modified since the last run are added to an archive, without replacing or deleting earlier versions of those files.

AFP: Apple Filing Protocol, the network file-sharing protocol used by Personal File Sharing.

archive: An archive is a copy of your files as they appeared at multiple points in time, sometimes stored as a single, larger file. Some backup programs use the term *archive* to refer to a backup in which the original files are deleted from the source volume after being copied to the backup medium.

client: A program that works with a server program is a client. For instance, Retrospect Client is a small program you can install on each of your computers. Retrospect Client communicates with the full version of

Retrospect on the server, which does the bulk of the work. The computer running client software is often called a client as well.

client-server: A type of network backup system in which client computers use a small background program to send files over a network without mounting a volume in the Finder. Backups are initiated by the server and stored on media connected to the server.

Combo drive: A Combo drive is an optical drive, standard on some Macintosh computers, that can read from DVD media and write to CD-Rs and CD-RW media.

data fork: Although this is less common in Mac OS X than in previous versions of the Mac OS, Macintosh files can be composed of two portions, a data fork and a *resource fork*. In general, the data fork holds data for the file—text, graphics, video, and so on—that could be relevant to any platform, whereas the resource fork stores information that's relevant only when the file is used on a Mac. (Often this information is ancillary, but other times it is quite important. For example, Classic versions of Nisus Writer store formatting in the resource fork.)

destination: The volume (hard disk, partition, optical disc, etc.) to which files are copied during a backup. Also called *target*. Compare with *source*.

differential: A type of backup in which each run copies all files which are new or modified since the initial full backup. Compare with *incremental*.

duplicate: A duplicate is a complete, exact copy of your entire hard disk that (if it's stored on, or restored onto, a hard disk) you can use to start up your computer if necessary. Sometimes called a clone or a mirror.

FTP: File Transfer Protocol, a common method of transferring files over the Internet.

incremental: A type of backup in which only files that have been added or changed since the last run are copied. Compare with *differential*.

local: Think of local as meaning "part of your computer." If you save a file to your Mac's hard disk, you are saving it locally. In contrast, you can save it *remotely* on a file server, which could be down the hall or on the other side of the globe.

media spanning: The capability of a backup program to split data (possibly even a single, large file) across multiple optical discs or other media—and rejoin them when restoring the files.

multisession: The ability to record additional chunks of information on a partially used optical disc as separate volumes after the initial write session. Some applications, including Retrospect, can add data to partially-used optical discs using a packet-writing technique; this does not create additional volumes, and it means that only the program used to record the discs can read them later.

NAS: See *network attached storage*.

network attached storage: Typically refers to one or more hard drives with their own Ethernet (or wireless) interfaces. Compare with *storage area network*.

off-site: When backup media is kept off-site, it is moved to a separate building from the one where the original data is stored.

optical media: CDs (including CD-ROM, CD-R, and CD-RW) and DVDs (DVD-ROM, DVD-R, DVD+R, DVD-RW, and DVD+RW). So named because they rely on lasers to read and write data.

pull: A backup initiated by a server, in which data is copied from a mounted network volume (a client computer) onto media connected locally to the server. Compare with *push*.

push: A backup initiated by a client, in which data is copied from a local disk to a mounted network volume. Compare with *pull*.

resource fork: Although this is less common in Mac OS X than in previous versions of the Mac OS, Macintosh files can be composed of two portions, a data fork and a resource fork. In general, the data fork holds data for the file—text, graphics, video, and so on—that could be relevant to any platform, whereas the resource fork stores information that's relevant only when the file is used on a Mac. (Often this information is ancillary, but other times it is quite important. For example, Classic versions of Nisus Writer store formatting in the resource fork.)

rotating archive: A backup scheme in which new or modified files are added to an archive incrementally (without overwriting recent versions), but files older than a certain date (or backed up more than a certain number of days ago) are removed to save space.

rotating backup: A backup scheme in which a complete copy of all selected files is made during each run, the newest set of files replacing the oldest of two or more previously copied sets.

SAN: See *storage area network*.

script: A set of instructions for a backup program to follow. Scripts may include source, destination, schedule, and other options.

server: A server is a program that sends information to client programs. Backup servers, for instance, work with backup clients to copy files from networked computers onto centrally located media. A computer running server software is also typically referred to as a server.

SMB: Server Message Block, the network file-sharing protocol used by Windows and Mac OS X's Windows Sharing. Sometimes referred to (slightly inaccurately) as *Samba*.

snapshot: A list of all the files in the designated folders at the time a backup runs. Backup software that uses snapshots generally enables the user to restore data to its state at the time of any backup with a single operation.

source: A source is a folder or volume from which data is copied during a backup; the data's original or primary location. Compare with *destination*.

storage area network: A device comprising one or more hard drives able to be shared among several computers, generally via high-speed FireWire, Fibre Channel, or SCSI connections (without using a conventional Ethernet-based network). Compare with *network attached storage*.

SuperDrive: An optical drive, standard on many Macintosh models, that can write to and read from DVD-R media and CD-R or CD-RW media.

synchronization: The process of maintaining identical copies of a file, folder, or volume in two or more locations.

verification: The process by which a backup program confirms that each copied file is identical to the original.

Index

Real World Mac Maintenance and Backups Periodic Task Checklist

You can cut out this page and hang it in a conspicuous place to remind you which tasks you should do when. You might also consider adding daily, weekly, monthly, and yearly reminders to your favorite calendar application.

Daily Tasks

✓ Back up changed files.

✓ Download (but don't install) software updates.

Weekly Tasks

✓ Clean up your Desktop.

✓ Back up everything.

✓ Rotate backups offsite.

✓ Use Software Update to install Apple software updates.

✓ Check for third-party software updates.

✓ Reboot if performance seems slow.

✓ Consider clearing certain caches.

Monthly Tasks

✓ Empty your Trash.

✓ Use Disk Utility's Repair Disk feature.

✓ Clean your screen.

✓ Clean your mouse or trackball.

✓ Exercise your laptop's battery.

Yearly Tasks

✓ De-dust your Mac.

✓ Clean your keyboard.

✓ Clean your iSight.

✓ Make archival backups to DVD.

✓ Remove unneeded files.

✓ Change your passwords.